PILLARS OF SUPPORT

Lessons to Help Parents and Mentors Form Trusting Relationships with Kids That Last a Lifetime

by Scott Whitehead

The names and identifying details of the stories in this book have all—except when indicated about friends and family members with their permission—been altered to preserve confidentiality.

Published in the United States by Chateau Books, Atlanta, GA

ISBN: 9781088064351

Cover design by: Zoe Norvell

Book design by Diana Wade

www.pillarsofsupportbook.com

Table of Contents

Foreword

In June 2003, I had the good fortune to join the staff of Peachtree Road United Methodist Church in Atlanta, Georgia. The church is located in the heart of Buckhead, which is a thriving community filled with highly driven and successful people. The appointment was not for the faint of heart, but as a native Atlantan, I was excited to be serving in my hometown. As a young pastor, I was eager to prove that I was up to the challenge and worthy of the opportunity.

One of the first people who came to visit my office was Scott Whitehead. Pastors are trained to be skeptical of those who are among the first to request a meeting when we arrive as they often have an agenda! However, Scott's smile lit up the room, and his calm and casual nature immediately put me at ease. It turned out that Scott's only agenda was to welcome me and get to know me. What I did not fully realize in that initial interaction was that Scott had decided that I was going to be one of his mentees, albeit one slightly older than his usual beneficiaries! Now, almost twenty years later, he remains a trusted adviser and dear friend.

Scott and I share a passion for engaging in the lives of young people. As I was finishing seminary, I served as a youth pastor in Calhoun, Georgia. That experience and those relationships remain among the most fulfilling and memorable of my ministry. Part of what makes Scott such a successful mentor for teens is that he is a kid at heart! Scott loves to have fun and derives joy from helping others discover their passions and purpose.

A few years ago, Scott invited me to speak to one of his small groups, which met weekly for breakfast. These young men got up early to cram in a back booth at the local bagel shop to hang out with Scott. While I cannot tell you what I said, and I doubt any of the attendees would remember either, I was struck by how Scott knew details of what was going on in each kid's life. There was plenty of banter, laughter, and then, final sips of coffee and juice before the mad scramble to make it to school on time. As we watched the final student scurry out the front door, Scott turned to me with the same smile that had greeted me when we first met many years prior. It was the smile of a man who understands the power of presence.

One of the many pieces of wisdom in the pages that follow is for parents to seek counsel from other parents whose children are just ahead of their own. Shannon and I were so lucky that the Whitehead children were just a few years older than our son, Zach. We learned so much from observing how Scott and Tasha navigated the various stages of parenting as they raised two amazing young adults.

As I read through these pages, I can hear Scott's voice in them! His distinctive style and delivery are evident in the instruction and illustrations. The insights that he shares from his many years of investing in teenagers are simple, but not simplistic. In an increasingly complex and chaotic world, Scott helps us return to the basics: faith, family, and friends. He reminds us that time is our most valuable resource, which requires us to be intentional and disciplined with how we spend it.

—Charles Z Gardner
Founding Pastor, Redwood Church
Atlanta, Georgia
February 2021

❖❖❖

It is safe to say that Scott is a man of action. By this, I am not referring to his crack-of-dawn wake-up schedule, or his need to constantly be moving. The type of "action" I am referring to is his ability to take an idea, or even something that is said, and make it real. This action is best exemplified through Scott's spreading and educating of Christian values.

The Bible tells us that no matter who we are and what we do, God has a plan for us. Scott has such a unique gift in that he can take the message of God's plan and show you that it is 1) very much true, and 2) not impossible to make that plan a reality. This is where the domino effect of Scott's talents come in to play.

Even after Scott uses his intellect, humor, and spot-on communication skills to get someone to truly believe that God has a plan, he does not stop there. In fact, for him, the task has just begun, and his ability to put things into action ignites. Scott, in the truest sense of the phrase, is a "people's person." Now you could go through all the 24,000 contacts in his phone or scroll through the 10,000 connections he has on LinkedIn to see this is true. Or you could hang out with him in a room for a measly five minutes and quickly see what I mean. Unlike most people with this type of personality, Scott does not use this to put himself up on a pedestal or to show everyone how spectacular he is. No. Scott uses his "guys' guy" personality to lift those around him UP. At the drop of a hat, Scott will leverage the same vast network of contacts to see if there is someone he knows that can assist someone else with their goals or aspirations. Scott does not do this to take credit for anything or to seek any sort of recognition. He does so out of the pure kindness of his heart and his love to see others succeed.

Scott is the best friend any person could ever dream of having. He is the man we should all strive every minute of every day to be more like. At the end of the day, if we have done something of enough worth to be mentioned in the same conversation as him, we have truly done something right and just.

Love you, Scott!

—Connor Larkin

Introduction

If you've picked up this book, more than likely you're facing some questions about your responsibility as a parent or a mentor. Do you find yourself wondering what role you should play in your child's life? Do you wonder if what you do or say can really influence a young person?

The answer is obviously, yes, you can make a difference.

What you do as a parent or mentor helps lay a foundation of love, security, and self-confidence that young people need to grow into healthy, loving, compassionate, and successful adults.

My first glimpse into just how much influence an adult can have in a child's life came years before I became a parent myself. When I was a young man just starting my career and living in Charlotte, North Carolina, I found myself with a lot of time on my hands. Sure, I was busy with work, but my social life wasn't as full as it had been when I was in college. Looking for something to do, I signed up for the Big Brothers program, and they matched me with eight-year-old Aaron. The first time I met with him, we went to get ice cream, and I started out just asking him basic questions about school and what he liked to do. Then suddenly, he blurted out, "I hate my father!" It turned out his father was an alcoholic.

I was stunned. I didn't know what to do with that emotion. I took him home, said goodbye, and wondered whether I was even cut out for this mentoring role. But the next week when it was time to hang out with Aaron, we had a great time. Week after week, we got together and talked, played ball, did homework, and just enjoyed each other's company. When he told me, "You're so much better than my dad," I clarified for him what a Big Brother relationship was. My role was to support him, offer advice on his day-to-day problems, and have fun with him.

Three years later, I moved to Birmingham, Alabama, for a job change, but I didn't want to disappear from Aaron's life, so I flew him down for beach vacations with my family and sent him to Space Camp one summer in Huntsville, Alabama. Despite my best efforts, without the intrinsic combination of time, support, and reassurance of my belief—or, more importantly, his father's belief—in his abilities, Aaron was unable to let go of the anger and frustration he felt regarding his absentee father. His grades in school suffered, he got into drugs when he was sixteen, and he then began selling narcotics. He unknowingly sold to a federal investigator and ended up in prison for a year. When he came out, he had lost any sort of self-respect, cycled downward again, and ended up back in prison for another three years.

While there, he wrote me a letter. He said he had begun to participate in church in prison and the seed of faith had been planted in him. His weight had ballooned to 350 pounds, but his newfound belief in God had encouraged him to take better care of his body. He started exercising and eating right, and when he got out of jail, he got into the fitness and supplements business. What surprised me was that even after all those years apart, Aaron had turned to me for help and advice. He didn't trust many people, but thanks to those early times together, he found trust in me, and I believe that the early relationship we formed helped him when it came to building a relationship with God and finding a way out of his drug use.

I invested in Aaron's business, knowing he had the will and drive to succeed. We are still in touch to this day.

I met Scott through United Way Big Brothers Big Sisters program. I'm now thirty-eight years old and we still keep in touch. He is my Big Brother.

He would take me to do a lot of fun activities and we always ate well. He always took me out for fine dining on special occasions and would even do cool stuff like renting limousines for my birthday. His family and friends always treated me like family.

We would go to Panama City, Florida, during the summer to Scott's parents' condo and yacht at Bay Point Marina. I have so many good memories from there—from the offshore fishing trips to riding Jet

Skis and riding the motor scooters. It was a blast!!

I took the wrong route in life in my teenage years when I was around seventeen years old, but Scott always stood by me and helped me any way he could. When I decided to get my mind right, Scott helped me start my business that I'm still running today eight years later. I'm forever grateful for his help.

I was a groomsman in Scott and Tasha's wedding, which was really cool!!

Scott taught me a lot about life from the importance of good grades, good manners, how to treat others, accountability, and the importance of being a good person. Scott has affected my life in so many positive ways.

—*Aaron*

That experience with Aaron was only the first of many relationships I've built as a mentor to kids over the years. From being a Big Brother to becoming a youth adviser at my church to mentoring at a halfway house for incarcerated young men, I have enjoyed being a positive influence in kids' lives, especially at the times when they're most in need. My ability to mentor was a trait that my mother recognized in me from a young age, when she noticed that I was good at giving a hand up to a kid who was struggling. I've been able to use my talents in working with kids through coaching, tutoring, and volunteering with community organizations.

Probably my most important role came when I became a father to my two wonderful kids. I am so blessed to have had my wife,

Tasha, as a great partner in that parenting journey, and our own parents both set great examples for us. Together, Tasha and I navigated the years of building faith in little people, creating relationships with them, instilling in them self-confidence and belief in their abilities, and setting expectations for their behavior.

I vividly remember when my parents told me that they were leading a confirmation retreat over my thirteenth birthday weekend. What? I thought. I was turning a teenager and they were leaving for my birthday? I felt like they were overlooking both me and the significance of this birthday.

Little did I know, my parents were planning such a big surprise birthday weekend for me the weekend before. I still look back on it and smile. When I came home from school with my friend Anna that Friday, we saw a massive waterslide in our front yard, with all of my neighbors there to celebrate my birthday. I had the biggest surprised look and smile on my face. They did not forget; they went out of their way to still make this the best birthday!

They were not done there. The next morning, I woke up thinking it was a normal Saturday; my brother and dad were supposedly going to Home Depot while my mom and I went to run errands. My mom wanted to go get some cookies for my dad, but she ended up taking me to ANOTHER surprise party with all of my school friends, with my dad and brother taking pictures of my once again surprised look and huge smile on my face. In addition, me and all my friends went to get our nails done after, and everyone went out to a nice dinner.

All this to say is what I thought was going to be the worst birthday ever with my parents being gone turned into the most memorable.

Yes, this was such a big event for me, but even when my parents came to my sporting games or my dad surprised me in elementary school for lunches—it all brought us so much closer. All those times my parents came to see me at school, on the field, or at performances in my early years of my life led me to be able to open up to them—about issues with friends, teachers, or any of the hard times in my life. I knew they were always going to be by my side and help me through whatever hurdle might come my way.

—A. Whitehead

As children, we were always encouraged, not nagged. We were told we could do something, not that we had to, and we were told our expectations, and not what we weren't allowed to do. I think these are some of the most important things our parents did for us. When you tell a kid exactly what they can or can't do or you ride them until they do something, they are not going to want to do it. This is true in getting them to play sports, going to church, etc. For example, when we were little, our parents set the expectation that we had to play one sport in fall and one in spring. They did not force us to play any specific sport—we got to pick that for ourselves. As a child, having a sense of control drove us to want to do something, not have to do something. No matter how old we are, this principle still applies.

—P. Whitehead

Through my years as a mentor, youth adviser, and parent, I've had many parents come to me with questions. Sometimes they'd approach me about mentoring their teenager, and other times they'd ask for advice in dealing with specific issues. They knew I had experience and felt like I might be able to share some of my own knowledge and experience. Those informal conversations grew into speaking opportunities about parenting and mentoring in front of large groups around the greater Atlanta area.

This book is the culmination of that shared advice. I have found that six major factors help young children grow into successful, well-adjusted adults: Trust, Relationships, Belief, Faith, Expectations, and Time.

Relationships. Whether between you and the child, the child and other adults, or the child and their peers, relationships are an integral part of our human experience. This chapter covers some ways to create good relationships that will build up children and help them grow stronger.

Trust. This concept underlies all the others. Without trust, you can't have a good relationship or teach your children about faith. Creating trust between you and your children starts from the day they are born and lays the foundation that underpins their entire lives. For mentors, it starts on day one of your shared experiences.

Belief. Having self-esteem is essential to success. When parents and mentors show kids they believe in them and will support them through good times and bad, it grows confidence within our kids.

Faith. None of us work to our full potential when we go it alone.

Belief in God will help you reach your full potential, and this chapter explores how to foster faith in your child.

Expectations. Once you've set a good foundation by laying the groundwork with strong relationships, trust, belief, and faith, it's up to you as the parent or mentor to set expectations for your child. More than just discipline, expectations are a compass that help guide your child as they set out in the world on their own and make life-altering decisions.

Time. None of what I cover in this book can be accomplished without investing time. Spend time with your child by participating in activities, having conversations, and living life with them. If I had a dime for every time I've heard a parent say, "I'm just too busy," I'd be a rich man. We're all busy, but we must not be too busy for our children.

In order to give some real-life examples for the reader on the importance of mentors and parents in their lives, we have asked a number of mentees and my kids for their interpretation of what the mentor/parenting relationship has done for their lives (edited only for clarity and brevity). The impact a mentor or parent can have in the life of a kid is boundless. I believe that I am using the gifts that God has given me to not only relate to these young people, but to have the energy and drive to mentor these kids. It's an important role in my life that I value.

I'm NOT a psychologist or parenting expert, but I do have years of experience in building relationships with kids from all backgrounds and at all different stages of life. I've learned a lot from my own journey, and I hope that in sharing my experiences with you, you'll be able to strengthen your own relationships with the young people in your life.

When I was younger, Scott was just a friend of my parents, a coach, and the parent of a good friend. It wasn't until I began to see the worst of times that Scott emerged as a mentor and a friend.

My junior and senior year of high school were full of highs and lows. During that time, I quit football, which led to a tenuous relationship with my best friends. My high school girlfriend and I had split up, I had been suspended for drinking at prom, and my mom had been diagnosed with breast cancer. Prior to all of this, I had begun meeting with Scott because he had seen a leadership role in me. Scott wanted me and a few of my buddies to take charge and be leaders of the football team. However, I wanted to focus on baseball because it was my true passion, and I didn't care to continue playing football.

After I quit, senior year was when I began dealing with a lot of adversity. I started meeting with Scott for breakfast, to discuss my situation, my relationship with God, and my future. At the time, it was a lot for me to deal with and I tried to avoid thinking about the reality of my mom's diagnosis. I remember having a conservation with Scott about how I didn't want to open up about those feelings to my mom, and Scott persuaded me to have that conversation with my mom. I finally worked up the strength to have the conversation and it was one of the best things I could have done. I felt like everything that had been building up over the last year was released. I make sure to call my mom every single day, no matter where or what I am doing because I don't want to ever hold my feelings from her again.

Scott and I continued to meet throughout senior year, and I was extremely nervous about getting into the University of Georgia. I had been waitlisted, but I worked the hardest I had all of high school to take five AP classes and finish with my highest GPA senior year. Scott was there to help me and keep me motivated and focused. He helped me to learn from those mistakes and grow into a better person. Scott and I have become closer and closer as we have traveled with the family and worked together, and even though I am in college now, I feel like our relationship has continued to grow. Scott makes every effort to continue mentoring and befriending those he cares about. He will drive hundreds of miles just to catch lunch if he feels like someone is down. Scott has been a great friend, a coach, and a mentor to me, and he and I both know that he was put here to do this for a reason.

—Chris

CHAPTER 1

Relationships

God has blessed you with a child and given you the responsibility to parent to the best of your abilities. Your duty is to develop that child's innate gifts and never let up on yourself as a parent. To do all these things, you first must build a relationship with your child. Through the years, you'll constantly work on that parent-child relationship to the point where it matters to your son or daughter beyond their childhood.

The hope is that even when a child reaches young adulthood and has the choice to be with their friends, they will still prioritize spending time with you.

Building Relationships from Day One

When you find out you're expecting a baby, a million thoughts run through your mind. Most of those thoughts are good ones, but honestly, some are terrifying. You might immediately picture crying infants, middle-of-the-night feedings, baby food, and high chairs, followed by visions of you changing diapers, carrying around those awkward, heavy car seats, hiring babysitters, and paying the exorbitant cost of daycare.

But then the sweeter parts of infancy come to mind—rocking at bedtime, dressing a baby in cute outfits and hats, bottle feeding, singing lullabies, laughing at bubbles during bath time, playing peek-a-boo and pat-a-cake, hearing the first laugh, or seeing that first smile.

An expectant parent's thoughts aren't limited to infancy. Many new parents worry about how they'll balance work and childcare, where they'll send their kids to school, and even how they'll eventually pay for college. All of these are very natural thoughts to have.

Parents have mixed emotions around every stage of life. Some love the newborn and baby years but dread the "terrible twos." Some parents can't wait for their child to start kindergarten, while others shed real tears when their little one climbs onto the bus for the first time. One parent can't wait until their kids reach middle school and they can start having some rational conversations around sports, politics, and current affairs. Meanwhile, another parent stares at the baby pictures wondering where that cute little kid went and who replaced him with that stinky, six-foot-tall, monosyllabic monster who consumes all the food bought and doesn't ever listen anymore.

Unfortunately, some parents use this reticence over one age or another to "check out" during those times, whether it's during infancy, preschool, or the teen years. You might hear someone say, "Aw, teen girls are really not for me. They don't want their dad in their lives then. I'll check in when there's less drama." Or a mom may say, "Ugh, my five-year-old just won't stop talking about Pokémon. He's driving me crazy! Is it wine night yet?" Another parent has a baby driving him so crazy that he prefers to be at work until his child falls asleep and the house is peaceful again. He doesn't mind signing up for the business trip because it means he'll have more time to himself without worrying about bath time, bedtime, and the clutter of baby gear all over the place.

The reality is that your child is always connecting to you, from that very first day. Those connections that build the relationship come through hearing your voice, being held by you, gazing into your eyes—all five senses connect him to Mom and Dad from the moment he is born, and the connection strengthens as the child grows.

If you're absent because you don't like a particular stage, think you're not needed, or are too busy at work, you risk diminishing the level and depth of the relationship that you can have with your child.

Those first five years are critical to let children know they're loved, nurtured, and a part of something bigger than them. Building that relationship early helps build a strong foundation of love between you and your kids. Part of being a parent includes setting appropriate guardrails—starting with the toddler years and on through middle and high school—and widening those guardrails as your child grows.

Growing the Relationship in the Teen Years

It's only natural for new parents to be nervous about what it takes to raise children and build strong relationships, but that focus shouldn't ease up as the kids get older. What happens when it's no longer easy to exert your will by counting down from five to stop bad behavior? Or when giving a time-out as a punishment no longer induces fear in your kid? Even individuals who grew up with an absentee or abusive parent and lacked a good example of how to parent possess a strong desire to get it right with their own kids.

One great resource for parents of teenagers is other parents who have paved the way. When my oldest child reached an age when we were ready to loosen the guardrails a little, my wife and I struggled with what was right. We knew people in our community whose kids were excelling and feeling confident, in a humble way, and those were the parents we asked for advice. For example, we would ask, "With this milestone coming up, we're thinking about a 9:30 or 10:00 p.m. curfew. What do you think?" Seek advice from parents who have gone ahead of you—but not too far ahead, because things change quickly. Perhaps you have a sophomore, and your friend has a senior in high school or a freshman in college. Ask them, "Hey, what did you do with Susan at this age? What were your rules? Because they've turned out in a way that I admire."

Why reinvent the wheel if other parents have gone before you with great methodology?

Develop transparency in your relationship with your teenager by communicating about issues as they come up and encouraging them to do the same with you so that the house stays free from strife. When your child has a good relationship with you as a parent, you're trusting each other, not as a ruler and subordinate, but as parent and child. The child doesn't get turned away when they come to you with a problem or a situation that is troubling them socially or academically. You're not going to know everything, and you don't need to know everything as a parent, but you certainly want to maintain an open dialogue with your kids.

One key to building a good relationship is to avoid putting your child in a position in which he's always feeling like *my parents are overbearing ... my parents don't trust me ... nothing I do seems good enough.* It puts your kid in a corner. He will begin to feel trapped and will find a way out. That way will usually be to rebel.

Note: If you haven't spent the time building an authentic relationship in the early years and your child is already a teenager, it will be difficult—not impossible, just difficult—to have parental influence. By that point, your child more than likely has given up on trying to create a relationship with you and is unlikely to respect your authority. It is not a kid's job to create that relationship; it is our job as parents. A child should always feel like that parental relationship is already present. It's a given in their eyes. But if they have struggled to create a relationship with you—continually asking you to participate in their lives and feeling rejected because it seems like you are too busy, superficial, or that most other things take priority over them—that creates a real problem that will be harmful throughout the teen years and beyond. However, I don't want parents in this situation to think there's nothing they can do. It's never too late; it's just much more difficult to start late. So start now. Start today.

The lessons I have learned from Scott over the years will always be part of my guiding principles in life. The one that constantly sticks in my head was a conversation over breakfast in the eighth grade. I had just been cut from the basketball team, despite giving what felt like my all. I was disappointed, discouraged, and did not feel like going to school that day to see all my friends who were happy about making the team. Scott pried the news out of me. He responded, "You have a whole year to get better and prove him wrong. Don't let someone else's choice hold you back from doing the thing you love."

These words had such an impact on my life: "Don't let someone else's choice hold you back." Whether it's walking down the hall hearing what people say about me, or not being invited to the "ragers" in high school, these words resonate. Scott was there for me regardless of what other people said.

I learned how to establish a faith in God, in a small classroom in church where Scott was my confirmation leader. It was there that I picked up that Scott himself was human and made mistakes, but through faith and a little effort, was able to rebound and become successful again, and he was content with where he was in life. The connections he has with other people shows me how to not only make friends, but keep them around. The daily check-ins, whether a Bible verse in the morning or a "good day?" text around dinner time has taught me to be honest and not hold things in. The unconditional support is something I value very highly—I switched cities, schools, and states unexpectedly over the course of two weeks. After I told him the news, instead of questioning my decision, the first words he said were, "I'm proud of you; this is a big decision and I will always support you." This was very comforting to hear. The friendship that we have has made a great impact on my life through faith, support, and teaching me how to stand up for myself.

—Patrick

Peer Relationships

The most common phrase you might hear from a teenager is, "I'm going to a friend's house!" For parents, it often feels like their teens are gone more than they're home. This is a developmental stage for a teen, and although you might feel second tier to them as a parent, it is actually a great thing—you want your child to start separating from you little by little and forming their own identity. Eventually, you want them to move out of the house and live on their own. Being out in the world as a teen with their friends is the first step in that journey.

Think back to your own teen years and how important friendships were to you. Now think about your children and how important friendships are to them now.

> ***It's very important for middle schoolers and teens to have relationships outside of the family, because they value feeling accepted, feeling wanted, and feeling like they're part of something bigger than them. Humans desire connection and acceptance.***

Sometimes, though, kids might hang around other kids who don't provide the best example of how to live a godly life. As parents, our job is to remain vigilant and know who our kids are spending time with. Also, our hope is that the deep relationship they have with us as parents will create in them an innate desire to hang around like-minded friends. And when they pick the wrong ones, the hope is that they will realize it quickly and take action to separate. Teens are at a stage in their development when they're seeking acceptance from outside the family, but sometimes it can be for the wrong reasons. That's where a good relationship and an open dialogue come into play. If you've instilled this in them that they are already part of something bigger, they won't need to seek acceptance from a transitory group of friends, because they'll already know they are accepted by family at a deep level.

While your teen is building relationships outside the family, your parent-teen relationship is still growing and developing. During this stage, you transition from Mom or Dad—the "superhero" who read stories, played ball, and gave time-outs and treats—to a person with whom your teen can have more big-picture conversations about life, love, the world, and their place in it. You begin to take part in activities you both enjoy together. When it's age-appropriate for that child (you will be the best judge of that timing), you can speak more freely about what *you're* going through and what you did back when you were a teen. Be more transparent when you're struggling in life. Talk with them when things are tough at work, when things are tough keeping the family going in the right direction and why, when things are difficult financially, or when you're struggling with your faith. Those kinds of conversations make you as a parent real to your teen and help strengthen your relationship. Otherwise, you may remain a distant, authoritarian-type figure. If you never seem to experience any stress or be affected by any issues big or small, how can they even relate to you? On the other hand, if you carry excessive stress and take it out on kids with yelling, anger, and hostility, they won't want to be around you.

Letting your teen know, appropriately, what is going on in your life is not burdening them with your problems or stresses. It humanizes the person they perceive as "having it all together."

Establishing a Mentor Relationship

In addition to the peer-to-peer relationships outside the family, teens should also build relationships with other adults during these formative years.

Mentors can be a great resource for kids in times of stress, or even for just sharing happy times together.

Allowing your child to have a mentor means letting someone else help you, and it's important for parents to support and foster those relationships. Whether it be a coach, teacher, youth leader at church, or orchestra conductor, so many people pour into our kids' lives every day. Those relationships can result in extra perspectives and illustrative stories that help bolster your child's worldview.

I first met Scott in the beginning of my sixth-grade year when he was the teacher for our confirmation class. When we went on the retreat for confirmation, Scott saw something in me that I didn't see in myself: that I was a leader. He tried to give me every opportunity to be one. Whether it was making me enter the talent show or letting me help teach a lesson in the adult worship, he always tried to help me realize and use my gifts as a leader. Soon after the retreat, Scott and I had breakfast in the mornings often and we talked one-on-one at church.

In February of my seventh-grade year, my dad was diagnosed with cancer, and it was a hard time for me and my family. I had my friends, but it's kind of weird talking about it with them, so I didn't. I got a text from Scott about two weeks after I found out, and he said that he was praying for my dad and that he would always be there for me. It was great to know that I had someone that I could talk to during this tough time.

Through a series of miracles, my dad has made one of the most incredible recoveries that the doctors at MD Anderson have ever seen. Looking back on it, I realized that of all the miracles that I had witnessed, I had missed probably the most important one. The miracle that I had missed was Scott, that he was there for me and always prayed for me and was always someone that I could talk to. Hang on to people like Scott—people that are always there in the good and the bad times, who always support you and try to make you the best you can be.

—Bobby

As a mentor, I'm always quick to tell a kid that I'm not his parent, and that's a good thing. Parents have the responsibility of disciplining and conforming their child to the rules of their family. The mentor relationship is different. Rather than being a disciplinarian, a mentor is a role model. I work with the kids I mentor to build a relationship of trust so they can come to me with just about anything that's going on in their lives and know that what we discuss is confidential and they won't be judged. Having that type of relationship helps build their confidence in other areas of their life, whether it's in academics, in sports, or socially. They have knowledge from someone who's been there and done that, and they can apply that knowledge and then come back and tell me if it worked.

I was invited to join Scott's Bible study when I was in seventh grade. I wasn't sure why I was going or what I intended to take from the lesson. I was nervous around adults and lacked self-confidence. For a while, I felt that his lessons did not really apply to me and where I was in life—I was too immature to fully understand their weight and meaning. But as I reached high school, all of his lessons began to really resonate with me, both personally and spiritually. It was through this that I developed the relationship that I have to this day with God. Scott allowed me to take my relationship with God down from an almighty power that I felt unworthy to speak to, to a relationship filled with love, forgiveness, and appreciation for all the blessings and things I had been taking advantage of in life.

A mentor is a role model. A role model can be a life changer.

Through these lessons and my time with Scott, I now pride myself on my ability to speak to my peers and adults respectfully and confidently. This is only one example of the many essential life tools I gained from my time with him, but one I am most proud of, one I thought I would never achieve.

—Mason

How do you build that mentor/mentee relationship? First, the child/teen must know you're there for them. They may feel like they're the only one on the planet who is dealing with the stuff they're going through. They get enough judgment every day of their lives—at school, in athletics, from friends and parents. They're judged constantly on social media. What's their status? How many followers do they have? All those different status symbols weren't there twenty years ago. With all those pressures and judgments, teens need a haven where they can be away from all that, where they can be themselves and seek solace.

I've had many different roles as a mentor. Many mentees have been participants in my Bible study at church, but I've also worked with athletes as a coach and as an advisor. On my office wall is a framed picture and note from two kids—my son and another kid—whom I coached in baseball for eight years.

To our Dads, Coach J and Coach Whitehead. Today we would like to thank you for all the years gone by, coaching us, encouraging us, when we couldn't catch a fly. You have taught us more than how to play the game, catch, throw, and run; you've shown us how to play with respect and dignity and have a lot of fun along the way. This year we hear will be your last, and we want you to know we'll remember all the fun times, from all the years gone past. Thank you from us and all the other players. We are glad you'll always be OUR coach when we really need you the most.

That letter was written by two twelve-year-olds who realized, after just a short amount of time on this earth, the need for that kind of relationship. They knew they had a lot of life in front of them, some of which would be fun and some difficult, but they had a relationship with two coaches/dads they could turn to when they really needed it. All kids deserve to feel the comfort that comes from having an authentic relationship with their parents and, maybe, if they're lucky enough, with a mentor.

When a child lacks a relationship with a parent, having a mentor is even more important. Building a relationship as a mentor might take four times the effort in these situations. It simply takes more time to help a kid without a foundational parent relationship to correct a bad trajectory in his life than it does to help a kid with a good parent relationship who is just being a bit rebellious and wanting to have some fun. Sometimes, your efforts as a mentor may come up short, and you may not be able to steer your mentee onto the right path. However, when a mentor succeeds in making a difference in a child's life and helps him choose the right road, the experience is as rewarding for the mentor as for the child. But the reward is not always immediate. It might be years after the mentoring relationship has ended that the then-adult mentee makes positive changes based on early foundations laid by a mentor.

Honest conversations are the key to building mentor/mentee relationships. One of the kids I mentor recently told me, "My curfew is still 10:00 p.m. Can you believe that?" I knew this kid pretty well and thought his good behavior might warrant looser restrictions at home, so I gave him some advice about how to talk to his parents.

"I'm not here to parent you, and that's their rule," I said, "but here's a way you can go back to your parents and talk to them about this curfew. Take the initiative of putting a game plan together and say, 'Mom, Dad, I'd really like to set up a time with you when it's convenient to discuss something.' First, that will blow them away and will change their mindset of what they're thinking about you. You know you've got a good, clean track record—you're doing well in school, have great friends, and hang around the right people. You've made a lot of progress in the past year, and I think you're in a place where you can nudge them to widen the guardrails. Tell them, 'I realize I've messed up in the past. But here we are, a year later, and I feel like my track record has improved. I thank you for that because you woke me up to the fact that I was doing some stupid stuff while I was trying to figure my life out. I've realized that's not me—that's not the direction I want to go in. I'm here asking for your trust. Can we move my curfew to eleven o'clock?' End with letting them know the minute you're late, they have every right to move your curfew back to ten o'clock."

Establishing a good relationship as a mentor helps you have those conversations. You're able to show mentees how to approach topics with their parents that they might think aren't open for discussion. You build your own relationship of trust with kids while helping them continue to build relationships with their parents.

However, at times, you may be mentoring a kid with such

inflexible parents that you know they will rarely say yes to what their child wants. In that context, you must help your mentee adjust to the situation. "How do we deal with this?" I often ask. "There are some things you can control in life, and others you can't. In your situation at this time, you might not be able to control the things you want, but if we can help you improve your relationship with your parents, you might find they give you more control over things in your own life."

I met Scott when I was in sixth grade and entering confirmation at my church. Scott was my confirmation leader and the first person I ever connected with at the church. The first fifteen minutes of Sunday school is meant for people to walk around and be social. My brother and I hated going to church on Sundays and wanted nothing to do with the social time. We would be in the hallway playing on our phones. Every Sunday, Scott would walk by and say, "Ah, I see we are being social again," and keep walking. My brother and I would laugh and think to ourselves, Why does he always say that? This routine started to grow on me, and I looked forward to Scott coming over to talk to us. He never forced us into the game room or told us to go be social; he just let us do our thing.

During our actual classes, what connected me so much with Scott was that he would give lessons in a way that a sixth grader would understand and be interested in. The greatest part about him was that he had worse ADD than any of the kids, so we never got bored during his lessons or zoned out. Scott made every lesson so relatable to the kids in my class that they would normally leave me thinking about my faith and my life. Throughout the remaining years at the youth program, you could find my brother and me wherever Scott was. We both went on to be confirmation leaders and went on the confirmation trip with Scott.

After sixth grade confirmation, one of my friends reached out to me about a Bible study. He said, "Y'all have to join this Friday morning Bible study. Scott's in charge and we meet at Goldbergs every Friday morning." My brother and I both thought, Friday morning? I'll pass. We hated getting up early, and the Bible study started at 7:15. But eventually, we thought, How bad could it be? Bible study is where I really found my faith and strengthened it. I was in that Bible study group from seventh grade to twelfth grade. Not only did it strengthen our faith, it gave us someone to talk to when life wasn't going so great. Scott could give you advice on anything. He knows everyone in Atlanta, so there wasn't much you could hide from Scott. I trusted Scott with my problems because I knew how much he cared for me and that he would do anything for me. Outside of your family, friendships like that are very rare.

I knew that when I told Scott my problem, he was going to do everything in his power to help me fix it. I can and always will be able to count on Scott for anything and knowing that has helped me open up to him over the past few years. He always tells us that no matter what we do, he is still going to love us, and that gives me all the confidence in the world to open up to him. With your parents it's different; they are upset with you and disappointed and will probably punish you. They still love you, but they don't always try to understand you. With Scott, he tries to understand you and always does because he puts himself in our shoes. Instead of getting angry, he asks you who you want to be and what kind of legacy you want to leave behind. That was always a powerful statement for me.

Did I want to be remembered as the kid who was drunk at every party? Or the one who everyone wanted to talk to? Thinking about these questions is what really motivated me to be responsible in high school and not be the kid getting into trouble every weekend. When I did get in trouble, I knew a text was gonna come from Scott: "Let's get breakfast." This was always a terrifying text when you knew you did something wrong, but a text I welcomed because I knew it meant he was just holding me accountable for my actions.

This year in May, I found out that my girlfriend I had been dating for a year and a half had cancer. She had a tumor in her knee and was going to have to do nine months of chemotherapy. The second I got the text from her, I broke down crying in my room. Once I caught my breath, the first person I called was Scott. I told him she had cancer and asked, "What do I do?" He calmly told me to be there for her no matter what and treat her the same as I always have. We are about three months into her treatment, and our relationship is still strong. Treating her like I always have has helped her feel normal, and when we are together, we both forget about all the bad going on and just enjoy our time together.

I love when my friends ask me who Scott is, because I get to say he is one of my best friends. They always look at me weirdly and say, "One of your best friends is an adult?" And I say, "Yes, he is."

—Devin

A mentor can step in and build a trusting relationship that helps a kid grow stronger in knowing who he is and in finding his own way in life, even when a parent hasn't developed a relationship early on with a child. Establishing a mentor relationship with kids who lack a strong parental relationship, however, can be a bit like walking a tightrope. In many such cases, the kids have frustration, anger, and pent-up energy that may result in real problems when you give them a little bit of freedom. It's easy for them to overstep the bounds they've been given and create family strife from their actions. Honestly, at this point, they don't really care anymore. Hopefully, by building a strong relationship with them as a mentor, you can show them someone does care and help build compassion within them.

For mentees who are harboring anxieties and fear, having a trusting relationship may help release that poison and bolster their happiness. Many of the guys I mentor have a hard time talking about their issues, but I say, "God didn't put us on this earth to be mute." Once you start talking about your issues, you gain confidence because you realize you can be honest and share your feelings with another and they will remain your friend.

Reputation is made in a moment; however, character is built in a lifetime.

I moved to Atlanta from Tallahassee, Florida. Being a baseball and football guy, I integrated into my new school's programs, where I met Scott—he was the football team's Servant Leadership Coach. With my luck, I was fortunate to break my collarbone in our first regular season game, resulting in an Instagram Direct Message from Scott wishing me a speedy recovery and letting me know when he was available for breakfast. Our first breakfast was a usual, "You're going to be the leader of the football team and I want to help you be the best that you can be. I am not here to be your friend, just to help you. And I already have enough friends my own age." At first my thoughts were: "Why the hell am I waking up at 5:55 a.m. every Tuesday morning if we're not going to be friends? Don't friends help friends? And fine, old man, I don't want to be your friend either. And I doubt you have enough friends." Childish of me, of course, but that's who I am.

So, breakfast after breakfast, 5:55 a.m. wake-up after 5:55 a.m. wake-up, Tuesday after Tuesday, Scott and I became closer. I saw who Scott Whitehead truly was being with that red hair: God's servant. Scott wanted nothing but the best for me. Scott was always there for me when I had a problem, but it probably wasn't easy given how little I truly opened up to him on some things. I was broken. I still am. I have had the perfect upbringing from perfect parents, with three amazing brothers and one amazing sister. One of my brothers, my older brother, passed away, making me the new ringleader of my favorite three kids younger than me. This took a toll on myself and my parents. My siblings were too young for the death of a loved one to know how it truly does affect you. I have learned to bottle things down inside and not talk about them. I tell myself I'm fine. Everything is fine, and it's going to be okay. That is how I've operated.

Until that morning on June 21, 2018, when we were having what seemed to be a normal breakfast, and after, proceeded to talk outside. That's where Scott told me, "You're the 'I'm fine' kid, and you can just bottle things up inside." Scott had told me what I had told myself for years when problems would occur. All the cards were on the table, and Scott had known who I was the second he met me. Scott wanted me to know that I can tell him things so he can help me and learn from actions that take place. He had for a while now, but he dropped the F-word (friend) on me again and it really hit home. We were friends. It was inevitable that this friendship would blossom. It was not forced, nor uncomfortable. He has helped me through countless problems. I have even helped him through some of his own. He showed me that no matter what happens, he will always be there for me, and I need to talk to him about anything that comes to mind. Because just like the first time we had breakfast, he just wants me to be the best person and leader I can be.

—Harrison

Another way to build relationships with your mentee is to find a common interest. If you played football in high school, for example, and your mentee is into athletics, they'll immediately be able to relate to you on some level. But remember, you don't have to be exactly like each other or even like the same things A boy named Jeb and I got through our lack of commonality by joking about it. Jeb was—and is—brilliant. To say he was strong in academics is an understatement, and he was also gifted in the arts—acting and singing— areas I never cared about. We developed a relationship through the youth program at our church. I went to one of his plays, which he knew was a huge deal because I don't even go to the movies. We would joke about our relationship, and I would say, "Why do you even ask me my opinion? You're so dang smart. I don't even know enough about acting to give you any advice!"

He'd laugh and say, "Well, I don't understand your sports, but it doesn't stop you from talking about it with me! Why would you go put a helmet on and hit each other? That makes no sense!"

We developed our relationship through bantering back and forth. And I told you he was smart, right? He went to Princeton.

I wouldn't say mentoring a kid is 100 percent not doable when you don't have things in common, but it definitely helps if you have an easygoing rapport.

Finding a Mentor

Now that we've established the importance of mentors in a child's life, just how do you go about finding someone to work with your child?

A few routes are obvious. If a kid is involved in church or a faith-based organization, plenty of options are available. Find a small-group leader at your church or synagogue or a leader at a local Young Life group. A good youth program will have people who are involved for the sole purpose of devoting themselves to kids' lives, either in a small-group setting or one-on-one.

Another avenue for finding a mentor is athletics. Good coaches coach not only because they love the game but also because they want to give back. Sports are a great resource for finding a mentor for athletic children.

As noted, a big part of finding the right mentor is finding commonality somewhere. For instance, if you have a singer in the house, you can't go to the football coach. A lot of the kids in my mentor group love business, and we connect because of that. They also know I love football and was a decent student who went to youth group and became a business owner. They realize I'm a guy who's already done this stuff, so I must know what I'm talking about.

As a parent, try to work behind the scenes with a mentor. The last thing you want is for your child to feel like Mom thinks he needs a mentor. It's a much better feeling when someone reaches out and your child thinks, *Wow, this coach is noticing me!* You can be behind the scenes discussing things with this mentor, but it's up to the kid and that person to connect.

Sometimes a mentor relationship can create feelings of jealousy in a parent. You may feel that when you give advice to your child, she doesn't hear it, but when her mentor tells her the same thing, it's suddenly the wisest idea she's ever heard. That's a natural reaction

Don't feel badly if you think your child could benefit from a mentor in his life—it doesn't mean you've failed as a parent. In fact, if you weren't doing a good job and didn't care about how your child was doing, you wouldn't even be thinking about looking for a mentor for them, and you certainly wouldn't be reading this book.

in kids, and it's another reason why having a mentor relationship can be helpful.

For example, I once had dinner with a mentee's father. He said, "It's interesting to me how on school days, we spend an hour and a half getting Patrick up and ready for school. It's a constant struggle with lots of motivation needed. And yet, when he overslept the day you were picking him up, he was in your truck in seven minutes, because he knew you were going to leave him if he was not on time. I don't understand what the difference is?"

"The difference is, that's the beauty of a mentor relationship," I said. "A parent is supposed to be there, and they know that, because you've been there all along. But what I have with them is new and different. Please know that you're one hundred times more powerful in that kid's life as a parent than any outside person can ever be. Your son knows I will drive away if he doesn't make it on time. You won't."

It can be frustrating to see your child respond immediately to something the mentor, coach, or teacher suggests when you've told them to do the same thing hundreds of times before. But use the mentor's influence with your child to your advantage: If you're unable to make inroads on a particular issue with your child, I encourage you to reach out, send a text, and let the mentor know. Personally, as a mentor, I will make sure to weave the topic a parent wants to get across into my next conversation with the child in a clever way and see if I can make some progress. Other mentors ought to be able to do the same.

Be a Living Example

As I said before, many of the guys I mentor relate to me because they like business and want to be successful at it, but it's also a good platform from which I model larger life lessons.

My choice of vehicles happened to be a good way to teach some of these values to one of my mentees who was into cars.

"Why do you drive that truck?" he asked when I picked him up in my Ford F-150.

"Because I love it."

"Why don't you get a Maserati?"

"Because I don't need a Maserati."

"Well, you can afford one."

"How do you know? And if I could, it's not a priority for me. My truck is perfect for me."

As an adult in a child's life, whether you're the mentor or the parent, you're a living example. My choice of vehicles shows my values—I don't need or want a new car every other year in order to show my success. You don't have to go into debt and pay high interest rates to prove your worth.

This is just one of many different little life lessons I might happen to share, and it might spring from a random conversation about car choices. My perspective might be entirely different from the one my mentee's family might have, but it could ultimately influence them in a positive way to see the issue from both sides.

A Cautionary Tale

I met Daniel when he was sixteen years old and living at Mountain Top Boys Home, a Christian group home in Northwest Georgia for kids who have come out of juvenile detention. Twelve boys live there with house parents.

Daniel had come to live at Mountain Top after a series of sad events. He was living in a mobile home with his parents and three siblings. One day, when he was fourteen, though they had no electricity or running water, his parents came home with a twelve-pack of beer and a small bag of marijuana. When Daniel confronted his parents about buying pot instead of paying the bills, his father said, "If you don't like it, get out."

Daniel went back to his room, which he shared with his three siblings, and packed two pairs of shorts and two shirts and left. He wanted better than what his parents were providing for him, but he had nowhere else to go. He moved under a bridge, in Chatsworth, Georgia, and worked whatever day jobs he could find to provide some income for himself. But one day, he stole a stereo out of a car and got caught. He'd started using drugs at fifteen, went into juvenile detention, and then ended up at age sixteen at the boys' home, where I served on the board. I also mentored some of those kids living there.

When Daniel and I met, I asked, "What made you do the things you've done?

"My parents."

"What do you mean?" I asked.

"My parents were so about themselves and so caught up in substance abuse that me and my siblings had no relationship with them. I realized that it was never going to happen. So, I left, not really knowing how to fend for myself. I was on my own."

After he left the group home, Daniel called me every four to six months to catch up. At age twenty-one or twenty-two, he fell head over heels in love with a young woman.

"Tell me about her," I said.

He told me that she already had three children by three different men. None were in the picture anymore.

I said, "Daniel, I'm a little concerned that it's going to be difficult for you to get into a relationship with a woman who is very accustomed to having children and not staying with the dad, or the dad leaving. It seems like a lot."

"But, Scott, I feel loved."

"I understand and I want that for you," I said. "I just want you to be careful."

"Yes, but I want to have a kid with her. I want a baby who loves me unconditionally."

Daniel had never experienced unconditional love in his life from a parent, and he was willing to risk everything, even with an unreliable woman, to get it.

So they got pregnant, and a year into the child's life, the mom decided to leave Daniel and continue the life she had been leading before she met him.

That story illustrates that when a child lacks a relationship with a parent, he may continually desire for someone in his life to love him in the way he has always longed for. While Daniel sought to fill that hole by having a baby with an unreliable partner, others seek to numb the pain through substance abuse.

Daniel's case is an extreme example, but it shows the innate human need for connection.

During confirmation, we took a youth group trip to a camp, and whether it was luck or fate, I was assigned to Scott's cabin. I sensed

Humans have an innate need for connection. There are unhealthy and healthy ways of finding it. Good relationships with family members and mentors tend to point people to the healthy ways.

that he truly had a genuine interest in getting to know me and being a part of my life. Scott has always had the gift of seeing potential in others that they do not see themselves. At the time, I was unsure of my own abilities and believed that I would be unable to climb the rock wall. After several failed attempts, I looked to Scott for inspiration. He assured me of my abilities and encouraged me to try again. His words pushed me to reach the top of that wall with ease.

Scott and I have continued to develop our friendship over the years. After confirmation, we started a small Bible study that would grow and be attended for six years before we left for college. Scott was patient while I struggled to grasp the concepts of faith and God. Through this patience and with his knowledge, he helped me develop a strong faith. This faith, along with Scott's devoted friendship, helped me navigate my grandmother's failing health and eventual passing. He is someone to talk to about difficulties in life, and he is always there never to judge, even as I looked to unhealthy ways to deal with pain and grief.

From then on, Scott solidified himself as a pillar of support in my life, acting as both a friend and mentor, continually seeing potential in my life. As I developed a solid sense of character, he has given me confidence through his unwavering support in the man I've become. Although I have had instances of weakness and lapses in judgment, his guidance and friendship have been a constant reminder of my path and potential in life. Sometimes these weak moments require tough love, which he is more than willing to give. However, through all the years, I never felt judged as I always knew he had my own interests in mind.

Scott's influence and guidance in my life is far-reaching. I have followed a similar path to him, attending the University of Alabama, where he tirelessly vouched for me and my character. This just shows the depth of his loyalty and the effort he puts into relationships with those he cares for.

But I soon realized that Alabama wasn't a good fit for me. I was worried that when Scott heard that, he was going to be upset and disappointed in me. I should have known better, but I was too stuck in my own feelings about the situation. When we finally talked about it, Scott was nothing but accepting; he agreed with my decision and supported me through a transfer to Georgia State University, which just reinforced that I'd made the right decision.

—Jack

It's Never Too Late

It's never too late to build a good relationship with your child. I fully believe that it's important to establish a connection from day one, but if you missed out on those early years, all is not lost. Maybe you've had an awakening that allows you to see things differently with your child. Maybe it's one of faith, or perhaps you've had a setback in your life that has allowed you to see that all the things you've been chasing are not worth it. If this applies to you, go to your child, talk to them, and share your feelings.

The conversation may go something like this: "I have been about myself too much. I've been self-absorbed—I've been doing it not to harm our relationship, but in trying to provide and in trying to develop my career—but I've now realized it's way more important to have a relationship with you. I want to strengthen our relationship from where it is today. I want it to be 100 percent; that doesn't mean I'm going to be overbearing, and that doesn't mean

I'm going to try to run your life. I just want to grow that so that in the last few years you have in the house, we can be closer."

The older the child is, the more difficult it might be to have that conversation, and the more you may need to prove you mean it. Younger children will be more willing to say, "All right! Let's go!" But the older ones will really question you, because they've been trying for sixteen or eighteen years to have a relationship with you and have gotten nowhere.

Kids can read right through a lie or see when you're saying something you don't really believe. Prove what you say through your actions. Those actions can be as simple as showing up to a baseball game or a school concert if you haven't done that in the past. Or sit down and have breakfast with your kid. It doesn't take much. Then keep it up, and continue to do more. You'll see a change, and they'll know you mean it.

It's never too late.

When Relationships Go Right ...

Being a mentor and being a parent are two totally different styles of relationships, but in the end, the outcome is very similar.

As a parent, strive to build a relationship with your child in their first eighteen years. When she graduates from high school and is ready for the next step—college, vocational school, or a job—she can enter the next phase of life knowing she can always rely on you. She's become self-sufficient.

If you do parenting right for the first eighteen years, your reward will be an amazing journey with a true friend for the rest of your life, because your child will cherish the relationship you've worked so hard to create.

CHAPTER 2

Trust

Trust is the linchpin of everything we do as parents, mentors, and role models. Trust means conveying to a child that you're there for them, no matter what might happen. Trust means you've created a safe space for them to come to you, in good times and bad, without judgment or fear. Our goal as parents or mentors is to help children grow into responsible, capable, compassionate adults. Naturally, you will make mistakes along the way, but if a foundation of trust exists between the two of you, you can overcome those mistakes, forgive any failures, and achieve outstanding results.

Trust underlies every concept in this book. Trust in each other is necessary to build strong relationships, to establish expectations, to convey faith and values, and to create an atmosphere where your child wants to spend time with you.

Building trust doesn't happen overnight.

Through our actions and words, we show our children that we support and love them. That love builds trust. In my work with young people, I've learned that it can take months, even years, to reach a point where a young person feels completely comfortable with me and is willing to share their fears and worries.

My friendship with Scott has had an incredibly positive impact on my whole life. We had meetings during the week where he would help me develop my people skills and help me talk through problems that every first-year faces. Now that I'm a senior, we talk about more complex things like how to make correct choices, and college, along with life after college. I know he wants the best for me and will do whatever it takes to see me succeed. He has helped guide me in my choices in the early years of high school and I could not be happier with how they've turned out. I believe everyone should have someone like Scott in their life as he has done a great deal to help me with mine.

—Joe

One young person told me it took two years before he realized he could trust me with anything. He said, "I had let you down a lot, but you never let me down. I didn't understand it at first, but eventually, I understood that's what a true friend was."

That is trust—a feeling that you're never letting a person down, in good times or bad. Trust is essential whether you're playing the role of a friend, mentor, or parent. People eventually notice when you're truly available for them with constant support, and they don't take that trust for granted. Instead, they appreciate it, and you've built a foundation that will last a long, long time.

When you're a parent, that process of building trust starts from birth. Along with your spouse, you have the ability to bond with your children from day one and be their provider of support. A mentor, on the other hand, must build trust from scratch, and that takes time. In my own practice, I like to share my own appropriate life stories with the kids I work with to help them feel like they're not alone in making mistakes. I let them know that I am not perfect. I trust them with information about myself, and eventually, they'll trust me with confidences about their mistakes and insecurities.

Eradicate Judgment

Building a foundation of trust in a relationship first requires creating a judgment-free zone. For many parents and mentors, this starts with managing your own expectations for the child. I have seen many parents and mentors enter a relationship with a child thinking, "I did this wrong in my own childhood, so I will never let that happen to them." However, starting with that thought process means you're unintentionally setting things off limits. The result is when the child slides into that gray area, they are likely to feel judged by you rather than supported. They may retreat from the relationship. Instead of trusting you, the child may begin to view you as an adversary. Create the space for a judgment-free conversation so they don't withdraw from you.

This relationship has brought out a new form of confidence and comfort in me that has changed the way I live. I've learned to be confident in the goals that I want to achieve and having support behind me the whole time has made this much easier. This relationship allowed me to truly express what is going on in my life without the fear of being judged or seen differently. Instead, I gain advice and reassurance that even when I've made a mistake, I can own up to it and work to fix them. The most important aspect of this relationship is that I have not only gained a closer relationship to God and my faith, but I have gained a lifelong friend who I know will always have my back.

—Bryce

Kids also perceive judgment through your tone of voice and the words you choose. For example, your child constantly leaves dirty clothes on his floor after you've repeatedly asked him not to. Your reaction when you once again find dirty laundry in his room is to say, "Why are you always leaving your dirty things piled around the room!?!" The result? He immediately gets defensive. He might pick up the clothes, but now he's doing it more from fear of the potential consequences. Another way to handle this situation may be to come to your child with a collegial approach rather than an adversarial one. "Hey, I've asked you to pick up your clothes a few times now. I just want you to understand that we are all a family and need to take care of this house together. This is one way I'm asking you to do your part."

I've had the opportunity to work with coaches on helping them build interpersonal relationships with their players. One day, I observed a coach's interactions with his players during a game. At one point, he told the quarterback to run pitch out to the tailback. Instead, the quarterback kept the ball and quickly got sacked. When he came off the field, the coach yelled at him—and I mean he full-on vented and shouted, with blood vessels popping out of his head because he was screaming at the kid so loudly. I watched the quarterback trudge to the bench looking like he felt completely humiliated.

"What was your purpose for yelling at that kid?" I asked the coach the next day.

"I wanted him to know what he had done wrong," the coach said.

"You know, that kid is every bit as smart as me and you," I said. "When he came off the field, he knew exactly what he'd done wrong. My guess is he wouldn't be your quarterback if he wasn't smart enough to know what to do. Yet you're tearing him down as a human being in front of his peers and fans. Instead of thinking about how to improve the next series, all he can focus on is the anger he has for you and negative thoughts about how he has not been able to do anything right."

I gave the coach an option for what he could do differently.

"Next time this type of play occurs, as your quarterback walks off the field, calmly walk up to him and say, 'What happened out there?' The QB will tell you exactly what he did wrong. Follow up with something like, 'We're not going to do that next time, are we?'

Give him the chance to take ownership of the situation and create a positive outcome with you."

We've all had experiences when a sullen teen has lashed out in anger or talked back in an insubordinate way. I recall a time driving in the car with my own son when he gave me some attitude.

Giving kids control of their own situation not only helps diffuse your anger but also helps you create an environment that's not as adversarial. It maintains the open, trusting relationship you've spent time building.

Immediately, I pulled the car over to talk with him. I wanted to be sure I gave him my full attention. I explained to him that it was his choice to use that attitude with me. However, if he continued down that path, the relationship between us would change. I would still love him, but I reminded him that our family had a set of expectations centered around respect and trust. If he deemed it unnecessary to show me respect, he would lose the privileges that came with a trusting relationship. You might have to explain to your kids that you'll still support them, just in a different way that they might not enjoy as much. My son, incidentally, chose to improve his attitude and keep things the way they had been for years.

Here's another example from a mentee's perspective:

The summer before my junior year of high school was when things really started going bad for me. My parents split up, and after my dad left, I started doing whatever I wanted without caring about the consequences. I was skipping football workouts, drinking every day, and staying out as late as I wanted. I ended up getting thrown in jail on Father's Day, but that didn't make me change anything. With my parents no longer living in the same house, I felt like I had the leeway to flaunt their rules and do whatever I wanted.

I think I hit rock bottom when I decided to quit the football team. When I got the guts to quit, the coach asked to talk with me. He said he was always there for me to talk to, but he thought there might be better people out there for me to talk to. The coach first recommended the school counselor, and I just laughed. Then he said he knew someone who worked with kids like me, and I knew exactly who he was talking about. At that time, I hadn't met Scott personally, but I'd been to some football leadership events that he led.

Scott texted me that night and canceled his Friday morning Bible study to spend time with me. That really made an impression on me. We continued to have breakfast together every week. It felt good to know I could tell him anything and he wouldn't get mad or judge me. He always had my back as long as I was honest with him. I started to change for the better, and he told me people had noticed. That made me feel really good.

Before I met Scott, I had a pretty bad reputation. I thought he wouldn't want to be seen with me in public. But I was dead wrong. He was there for me whenever I needed him. He helped me gain a significant amount of confidence in myself, and I started to care more about my actions and my future. He showed me so much about life that I wouldn't have learned without him. I can definitely say that Scott helped save my life. To this day, Scott and I remain very close friends, and he's always there when times get rough.

—Nic

Using a more positive tone, holding back your judgment, and giving kids some control over their outcomes are all ways to build and maintain trust. That trust is essential to strong relationships, setting and meeting expectations, and instilling values and beliefs.

Giving Room for Growth

If you create a solid foundation of trust, your kids will depend on your support and share their thoughts and feelings with you. They'll also have the security necessary to reach their goals and live up to their full potential.

One teenager shared with me that the best conversations with his parents were the ones where they focused on his potential. "It helps me feel good about myself when my parents tell me they're proud of me and excited about my future," he told me. He was

> ***Healthy, positive relationships provide the energy people need to succeed, while toxic relationships zap energy and leave people feeling depressed and listless.***

working in a store where he helped a lot of his parents' friends, and often they would tell his parents how polite and helpful he had been, which made his parents proud.

On the flip side, he felt frustrated when he made a mistake and it seemed like his parents constantly brought it up. Years after an incident had occurred, his parents still used it as an example of why they worried about him and his future. It's unproductive to harp on past mistakes; in fact, most therapists advise against it because in doing so, you convey a lack of trust, even if that's not your intention. Instead, work with your child to figure out a way for them to avoid repeating the same mistakes. I'm a big believer that failures in life are always opportunities for growth, and in a trusting, supportive relationship you can work with your kids to turn their negative situations into positive ones.

Much of growing up is about figuring out who you are and what you're meant to do in life. Our job as parents and mentors is to foster an environment where children are encouraged to try new things, to reach outside their comfort zones, and to grow as people. One of the best ways to do this is through conversation. You've worked hard to build a relationship founded on trust, and within that trusting environment, your kids are comfortable coming to you with frustrations, stresses, and anxieties of life. When they do, use that opportunity to talk and actively listen to their troubles, and then provide a supportive response.

This growth and leaving the comfort zone can come when kids are choosing their high school classes and preparing for college. The decision of whether to take AP classes or college-level courses feels like life or death to many kids today. Society puts so much pressure on them to succeed, and they look at other students and compare themselves to their performance. Word gets around about a prototypical "Alex," who is taking seven AP classes and wasn't accepted to his dream college, despite his perfect résumé and leadership positions, and the sleepless nights set in for everyone.

Parents often ask me what they should do for their kids who are stressed out and anxious over AP classes and college admissions. My advice? Think about the big picture. What are they really trying to accomplish? Set some goals to work toward and find a path that's right for the individual teen. It's okay for them to do whatever is best for them as an individual if they're doing their best. It's not for you as the parent or mentor or anybody else to define them; an individual alone defines who they are. You are there to help guide them.

This attitude works in any situation, not just when it comes to choosing AP classes. The important takeaway is to sit down and have a conversation with your child. Help them figure out what they think they would like to accomplish in life and give them the support they need to make their goals a reality.

Your job as a parent or mentor is to convey to young people that they are unique and wonderful human beings. You'll be amazed just how much a child can accomplish with that confidence in them as an anchor.

CHAPTER 3

Belief

Building a good relationship with our kids is one of the key building blocks needed to help them grow into self-sufficient, successful adults. Another cornerstone is instilling a strong sense that we as parents and mentors believe in them and love them for who they are as an individual.

As parents and mentors, we help develop self-confidence in kids. We show kids we believe in them, and from that they learn to believe in themselves. Building that belief is a process, and it's important to lay the foundation early so it's in place when they begin to navigate the tough middle school and high school years.

Young kids often show a strong sense of self-confidence. For example, if you ask an eight-year-old what she wants to be when she grows up, she'll state clearly and without hesitation, "I want to be an astronaut." Whether the answer is fireman, archaeologist, doctor, or teacher, young kids believe in themselves and their abilities, as evidenced by their confident choice of future careers.

Once they get to middle school, however, fear hijacks their self-confidence. They feel like all eyes are on them, and they don't want to make the wrong move. Hesitancy and self-doubt start to emerge. Ask the same question about what they want to be when they grow up, and they may now answer, "I don't know, maybe a teacher?" Or they might not even answer at all. They're scared that they don't have the skills or the ability to attain or achieve a chosen career, or they're hesitant to say out loud what they'd really like to do for fear that other kids will laugh at them.

The good news is that if you've built a strong foundation of belief in them, kids can survive the struggles of middle school relatively unscathed and will typically regain some confidence in high school. But for those kids without people who believe in them, or for those who feel that no one believes in them, the struggles of middle school may put them in a tailspin that grows even worse in high school.

Building Blocks of Belief

What you say matters. One of the easiest and best ways to show

> ***Kids who feel they have nowhere to turn—no support network—will turn to their peers, and this unbalanced and untested group of folks are not the best ones to be doling out advice to your child.***

kids you believe in them is through what you say. Your carefully chosen words express belief in them and let them know you support them. Tell them when they've done a good job, compliment their outfit, congratulate them on a well-played game. Positive affirmations and expressions of love are so important, and you don't have to worry about going overboard. The worry comes in when you find yourself being too critical.

Too often, the words teenagers hear and remember are the negative ones. "Why isn't your homework done?" "Are you going to wear those shorts to school? They're too short." "Why didn't you write more on your book report?" "I don't really like your friend Susan; she's a bad influence."

Middle school and high school kids already feel like everyone is looking at them with a critical eye. When a parent or a mentor contributes to that criticism, it can be overwhelming. Criticizing a child doesn't mean you don't believe in them; however, depending on the child's age, it can certainly send that message, especially when the criticism is relentless.

Knowing that my parents truly believed in me—in all stages of my life—gave me the ability to be myself and do the things I love without

Kids who face constant criticism won't stop loving their parents—they stop loving themselves.

thinking about my parents judging or critiquing what I do. I knew they would support me no matter what sport I played or boyfriend I had. They might not like my decision, but they have all the faith in me that if I believe it is the right decision, then they believe it too. Since my parents never stop believing in me, it allowed and still allows me today to be able to open up to them about life. I know if they always were critiquing what I do, I would not be able to open up to them as much, because I would be ashamed to talk about my problems without them shaming and criticizing me. It really makes them my best friends, because we all get to listen to each other and be there for each other without any shame or judgment. I could not be more thankful that this is the relationship I have with my parents.

—A. Whitehead

Yes, it's important to choose your words wisely and avoid being overly critical. Verbal affirmations show someone you believe in them. Remember that kids sometimes act overly confident to mask or cover up insecurity. What they really may be searching for is affirmation.

Be quick to listen, slow to speak. Sitting back and listening is just as important as the verbal support you give a child. When they come to you with a question, don't be too quick to spout out a lecture for an answer. Instead, ask them some rhetorical questions. They may have their mind set on something, but take time to sit and listen, ask them questions, and give them feedback. This puts you in the position of a collaborator with whom they can work to find a solution. They'll see that you trust them and believe in them.

I used this technique quite often on my own kids. One day, my son and I were watching a baseball game when he was about sixteen. Out of the blue he said, "Dad, I'm going to go out to a party later on."

My first instinct was to tell him, "No," but instead I said, "Sure, you can go to that party."

He seemed shocked by my quick affirmative response. "But, Dad," he said. "You work with kids my age. Are you sure you want me going to that party?"

I said I did know. And I also knew my son. I told him I wasn't worried about him going, because I knew he wouldn't want to risk losing the respect of the kids in his leadership group, and he wouldn't want to be a bad role model for his younger sister.

Later, when the game was over, I asked him if he was ready for the party.

"I'm not going now," he said. By talking through things with me, he realized that, at sixteen, that kind of party wasn't where he wanted or needed to be.

Most kids are pretty smart. They know the difference between right and wrong, and they know the direction or path they should be taking in their lives, even if it isn't the path they're headed on at the time. Engaging in open dialogue, being asked rhetorical questions, and knowing they have unconditional support makes them reflect on their decisions.

One of my mentees might come to me frustrated that his parents are constantly against him, but after talking and thinking things through, we can break the situation down and get to the root of why his parents are pushing back. The teen will see he's going down the wrong path, which leads to an understanding of why his parents are putting up barriers.

For example, a ninth grader came to me after a big fight with his parents. He told me he wished his parents believed in him as much as I did. Without question, his parents believe in him—way beyond what I do—because they're his parents. But his behavior was such that he didn't give them time or reasons to compliment him or provide the positive support teenagers need. He would mouth off and then run to his room and slam the door and turn the music up LOUD. All the interactions between him and his parents became disciplinary, with no down time where they could sit together and have calm conversations.

The ninth grader thought his parents were disrupting his life and being control freaks. What he couldn't see was that because they believed in him so much, they were being hard on him. If they didn't care about him, they wouldn't bother to discipline him but would instead just let him run free.

My job as his mentor, through open-ended questions, was to help him see the big picture and understand that his parents did believe in him and support him.

Allow kids to accomplish projects and goals on their own. Just as it's important to help guide kids to work through their problems (mostly) on their own, it's also important to let them accomplish tasks, big and small, independently. This is especially true for older teens. If you've given them a job to do and then you step in and do it for them, it sends the message that you don't believe they know how to do it and that you don't believe in them.

Take something as simple as washing a car. Nothing is more degrading than completing the task at hand and being in the process of showing off the newly cleaned car, only to have Mom step in and fix a few places that might have been missed.

Encourage good peer relationships. When someone your own age believes in you, it boosts confidence and can really help kids out in tough situations. The flip side is that when kids choose to

It's important for parents and mentors to take a step back and allow for kids to do a job in their own way. Relinquish some control and be proud of a job well done, even if it's not the way you would have done it, and even if it's not perfect. It will show just how much you believe in that kid.

follow a bad role model, the results can be disastrous, especially when they're not getting support from adults and they feel as though the negative influence is their sole source of support. Kids who don't have someone at home encouraging them or someone like a coach mentoring them will look for support anywhere they can find it.

Start early with your child by giving them opportunities to invite peers to events with your family. It could be as simple as dinner or something bigger like a vacation. This gives kids confidence to build peer relationships and choose the right friends.

It's crazy to think about how a life-changing relationship with someone can start from just a single encounter. My good friend Charlie said that he had a mentor/faith leader who wanted to meet me, and my reaction was something along the lines of, "Um, I guess?" The meeting could not have turned out better, and over the last four years, Scott has been an incredibly strong source of support, faith, and love for me, as well as each of my friends that meet with him. But he took it further than that—teaching us to be better men. We have become the point of support for others around us. Bible study has always been something to look forward to each week, and although I'm sad it ends soon for us, I know that the relationships built and lessons learned will last a lifetime.

—Grant

Relate at their level. My ability to relate to kids and get them to open up didn't come overnight. When I first started leading a youth group, I was scared to death. At the time, I was a young father, and the last time I'd hung out with eighth graders was when I was in the eighth grade myself. I may not have had a lot of training, but I had purpose and passion, and with that passion came patience and learning.

It's important to let kids know you're not much different from them. They hear someone tell them twenty to fifty times a day, "Don't worry, you've got this." But to them, it's all white noise. They're scared and afraid to fail. I tell them, "Guess what? If you fail, you're just like me." When you open up to them and share your failures, they respect you as a person. It's also important to show that failing is a path to learning.

We all stumble at times, but it's only through failure that we learn how to succeed.

I like to think that being with kids is like negotiating a business deal. When I work with clients to negotiate a new deal, I always try to put myself on their side of the table, rather than sit across the table from them, at least figuratively. It allows me to understand their needs, figure out how to meet those needs, and plan how to create a better business situation for them. It's not about me winning and the client losing; it's about how I can help clients win because that means I win too.

The same is true for kids. Get on their side of the table to glimpse what they're going through. Try to view the world through their eyes and show that you're there to help them win.

When I first started meeting with Scott, I always knew he gave good advice, but I didn't know how it would help me later on. Around February, I was faced with a decision that many kids my age had to deal with, yet my scenario was more unique. At the time I had a choice to make, and for me it was a very tough decision. I had the opportunity to play college baseball, but I wanted to go to college and do the fraternity and normal student route. I would stay up many nights till 4 a.m. just thinking, What the hell am I gonna do? The toughest part of this was I knew I was letting my dad down if I didn't choose to play baseball. Whenever I told my dad, I could see the disappointment in his eyes and his words did not make me feel the best.

One phrase from Scott changed my life forever. "College decisions are the one time you can be thinking about you at that moment. Once you make the decision, it becomes about others again." I took this to heart and chose to be selfish, and I am already reaping the benefits from this. If it weren't for Scott, I could have had a miserable four-year experience.

—Nic

The Ability to Press Pause

As hard as we try to raise kids with strong self-esteem, it's only natural for kids to have doubts and anxieties. For some, this can lead to tragic consequences. A few years ago, the brother of a kid I knew committed suicide. Many kids I was working with at the time knew this guy very well, and they came to me with questions, which were the same questions we all ask ourselves when someone takes their own life. Was there anything I could have done? Did I miss some clues along the way? How did I not realize things had gotten that bad?

In times like these, I tell kids to remember three things. 1) There is nothing you could have done. 2) Take a habit, skill, or trait that you admired in that person and incorporate it in your own life to carry their legacy forward. 3) Time is going to heal your pain.

I often think that if a person who commits suicide could push the "pause" button right before they swallow those pills or pull the trigger and fast-forward three days to their own funeral, they would never go through with it. They would see and feel so much belief in them and so much love. That's the power of belief at a higher level.

All my life, I've lacked the ability to convince myself that people liked me. I started smoking, drinking, and having relationships with girls, anything I could do to impress my peers. I was only thirteen when I started smoking. When you're caught up in things that are illegal, your first instinct is to lie. I lied to my parents, to my family, even to my girlfriend at the time, to hide from the truth. Eventually the drugs caught up with me and I was confronted by my parents. Then Scott showed up at my door. He was able to be the mediator between my parents and me and helped me open up to the feelings I was experiencing.

Fast-forward to my freshman year of high school, and I thought things would be different, but they weren't. My girlfriend broke up with me, my parents were fighting all the time, and I didn't know how to handle my feelings. I was depressed and felt like pain was the only way to feel alive. I began to punch walls every time I was upset. I hit rock bottom when I attempted suicide. A that point, my parents admitted me to Ridgeview, a hospital for depression, and that was my wake-up call. Through therapy in rehab, I realized I'm in control of my own mood, and I can't let depression cloud my thoughts and feelings all the time.

One afternoon I had a visitor. It was Scott. It made me feel at home talking to a friend for the first time since going to rehab. He kept telling me I had purpose in life. At my darkest and lowest point, Scott showed up, and his words meant so much to me. After getting out of rehab, my relationships grew stronger, with my parents, my friends, and God. Through it all, Scott has always been there for me, and there's nothing I can do to repay him for what he's done for me and my family.

—Foster

A good foundation of belief doesn't cure everything, but it helps when you get to this stage, where you really doubt yourself, to go back and look at your mom, your dad, your sister, your friends. You've got people who believe in you.

It's up to us—their mentor or parent—to walk them through and help them see the amount of belief we have in them. Hopefully, they'll come to us if they're ever having suicidal ideations. Study after study has shown that a parent or a mentor talking about suicide with a kid does not encourage suicidal thoughts.

Work on the building blocks of belief in your kids. It will give them the ability to push pause and fast-forward or rewind to see just how much people around them care about them. Everyone has doubts now and then and suffers through down times, but with a good foundation of belief in them, an individual can find the strength to get through anything. Not to mention, the good news is when you are in a low … things are about to get better, so get excited!

Finding Purpose in Life

"Friendship" is the word that comes to mind when I think of Scott, and it's challenging to properly connect the words that do justice to the impact he's made on myself and so many. Invaluable lessons shine through from what on the surface looks to be talking over a simple cup of coffee together on Tuesday mornings.

The most important lessons haven't always been understood at the end of our conversation, but they click in over time. Most notably for me has been the distinction of "Desire" from "Purpose." Scott lives a life of Purpose, while the 18-year-old that grabbed lunch with him for the first time lived a life of Desire. On the surface, they look very similar. However, when you live a life of Desire, you always come crawling back depleted. You're never able to achieve, win, or reach that "next big thing" enough to fill the void that sits in you. Purpose, on the other hand, seems to grow stronger over time. It's a consistent reflection of who you are and continuously pouring that into the world around you. When viewed on a greater timeline, the difference between a life of Purpose and a life of Desire becomes glaring. Countless times Scott has told me, "When you discover your Purpose, your life radically changes. You fly out of bed in the morning, your conversations change, your relationships grow deeper. It shapes your life in a way that fills your cup up day after day."

Pairing closely with Purpose is the lesson that hides under the paradox of Joy. The misconception I continuously found myself in is that your Joy comes from the outside, or the fulfillment of that Desire. The reality reflected so consistently to me through Scott is that it never comes from how well the world loves you, but how well you love those in the world around you. The discovery of your true gifts and channeling those into serving and giving unto others, while expecting nothing in return, brings out that Joy. It's the Joy I see shine in Scott without fail every day. It's the lesson that isn't understood by the end of a single conversation, but on a greater timeline as the lesson becomes glaring.

I feel so fortunate to have a friend like Scott who asks for nothing but the opportunity to be there for me.

—Hugh

Helping a person believe in himself is a continual process that is just as important in the high school years as when kids are younger. Even the most self-confident kids will question their purpose in life and feel lost at times. They may think, *Why am I even here?* For instance, their childhood desire to be a vet may be dashed when they realize they can't stomach biology after the cow's eye dissection. The lifelong goal to play in the NFL might evaporate when he never gets off the bench of the JV football team. And the list goes on.

When a kid turns to you, three approaches may help them out of a slump and onto a new path.

Reframe the situation. This approach helps kids see things in a different, more positive light. Recently, I was working with a group of high school seniors on their résumés. I suggested to one teen whom I had known for a while that he should consider starting his

> ***It's rare that a kid with a goal at age five sees it fulfilled at age twenty; more likely, new goals are formed, new people are met, new opportunities arise, and a new path emerges.***

own business. He said no; he felt like he didn't have what it took to be a business owner. He didn't have confidence in his own abilities.

I suggested we look at things from a different perspective.

"But working for myself is a big risk," he said.

"But working for someone else is a risk as well, isn't it?" I replied. "If things don't go well with the company, they can give you two weeks' notice before laying you off. When you work for yourself, you're not at the mercy of a corporation. You control your own destiny."

That student lit up. He said he'd never thought about it that way before.

Reframing the situation helped him see things in a new light.

Put a mirror to their faces, figuratively speaking. Help kids see just how much they've already accomplished. When my son was a junior in college, he called me saying he just didn't feel like he was accomplishing anything. Here was a kid who had always worked hard and had a list of leadership accomplishments a mile long. He graduated from high school with a 4.0 GPA, was an Eagle Scout, and started three businesses before he'd even left high school. Once in college, he had worked at a private equity firm. Then, during his junior year, he decided to take a break. The problem was that his brain wasn't allowing him to take a break. All his life he'd been working and creating, and now he had begun to feel like he was drifting along without a purpose.

For his mirror, I held up his résumé from high school. I had highlighted all his accomplishments. Words like *founder, co-founder, leader*, and *Eagle Scout* all jumped off the page. "This is who you are; don't forget it," I said to him.

In talking through his feelings and looking back on who he was, my son realized he needed to get involved in something to feel purpose in life. Taking a break might have seemed like a good idea at the time, but it had left him feeling lost and aimless.

Even without a résumé in hand, you can hold that mirror up to a kid figuratively by asking what accomplishments give them the most pride. With a little prodding, they'll be able to tell you something, whether it's leading the marching band, teaching a class in Sunday School, or cooking up the best macaroni and cheese for a family gathering. Sometimes you might run into a situation where a kid really can't think of anything. In these cases, ask what their friends like about them. Are they a good listener? Fun to hang out with? Have great taste in music? Any of these things are qualities worthy of pride. Through that mirror, kids start to see what others see and believe in themselves.

Help them discover their gifts and find purpose in life by asking what they enjoy doing. Ask what activity makes them the happiest or have them think of something they can do for hours on end. For example, say a kid answers that his favorite activity is playing video games. He knows he can't make a career out of that, but with your help, he can identify his gifts from what he enjoys doing. Take his answer and push him to think further. What is it he likes about video games? Playing with other friends? That might mean he likes being with other people and working with others. Does he like figuring out new ways to compete? For these kids, their gift could be related to strategy and the ability to be forward-thinking.

This is another good chance to relate to kids by letting them know your own struggles. They might look at adults and think we've got it all figured out, but most of the time, we're trying to ascertain our purpose and gifts just like they are, and it's some-

It's eye-opening for kids when they realize that the hints to what their gifts might be are right there in the things that they already like to do.

thing that's always changing. I consider one of my gifts to be that I enjoy getting up in front of people and speaking, but when I was a teenager, the thought of public speaking scared me to death.

Throughout our lives we grow and change, and God will move us around to new areas where we can fulfill our purpose in life. One of the things that has always helped guide me is prayer. For kids who are trying to find purpose in their life, encourage them to talk to others, to explore their gifts, and maybe most importantly, to pray about it.

As parents and mentors, one of our key roles is to help instill a sense of self-confidence—of purpose in life—in the kids we're lucky enough to have a relationship with. Showing them that you believe in them as you help them find their path in life is one of the important foundations of a good relationship.

CHAPTER 4

Faith

As parents, we can do many things to build relationships with our children, show them our undying trust in who they are, and help plant self-confidence in them. But we can't do it alone. When you are mentoring or parenting children, it's important for both of you to acknowledge that there is a power greater than you in this universe. And having a relationship with that power—whatever higher power that might be for you—is essential in this life. It's a recognition that everything is sacred and connected.

In Latin, the word religion means "to tie together." In a faith-based community, we are surrounding kids with people who have faith in a higher power and are walking through life with that belief. When we connect with God, we step into alignment with a larger purpose for our lives. Please know that I am not advocating on behalf of one faith over another or pressing Christianity over Judaism, Islam, or Buddhism. However, as a Christian, I speak from that faith perspective.

Both of my parents have a great faith. Growing up, I saw how excited they were to go to church and worship the Lord. They never told me that I had to be a Christian, because they were going to support me no matter what I believed but they showed me what it was like to be a Christian. I saw that when they were in doubt or concern, they turned to God, and also when they were happy and everything was going their way, they turned to God. It really showed me how God wants to build a relationship with us and them modeling how to have a relationship with God. By the time I was in middle school, I was waking up very early on Sundays and pushing my parents out of the door to go to church. I loved being surrounded by people who have the same morals, values, and beliefs as I do so we can all grow in faith together just as my parents have shown me. I still chase after the relationship with God and seek Him for all advice because I know how impactful it is.

—A. Whitehead

One of the benefits of a faith family is socialization. Attending services at a faith-based organization like a church is a great way to socialize outside the family, outside of school, and in a different location with different people. Children receive age-appropriate religious instruction from someone other than their parent. The early focus is on explaining the religion in simple terms with songs, picture books, and coloring in Sunday school classes, and the focus shifts in the teenage years to small groups that discuss how faith can affect the choices you make with larger life issues, like dating, substance abuse, and college. Moments with the minister or participating in services—all of it helps get kids acclimated to that church or faith-based organization so it becomes the norm in their life.

Modeling a relationship with a power greater than you in a faith-based community must start early. I'd like to caution against a boring type of education and faith exposure that goes something like this: "Okay, kids, sit down and open up your textbook." To kids, that feels like the sixth day of classes after having been in school all week. Sunday school should be a high-energy environment led by somebody who is fun and who inspires them. It becomes their "third place" outside of home and school.

At a place of worship, you meet people both in your church community and out in the broader community, especially when volunteering. I've had the opportunity to volunteer alongside my youth group by helping stock a community pantry, manning a soup kitchen, and pounding in nails with Habitat for Humanity.

Serving means doing things that are about others and not yourself. It gets you out of your own ego and head and exposes you to the problems that exist in the larger world.

Faith is especially important as kids become teenagers. When I was thirteen or fourteen, I dreaded going to church on Sundays. I disliked it and thought going to church was the most miserable thing. I was done. But then I heard some friends of mine talking about their church, which happened to be across the street from mine. One day, I just walked across the street to check out their service, and I never left. I felt energized there. The little seed of faith that was planted in me grew and grew. My parents didn't insist that I attend their particular church; they knew that it was more important for me to feel happy and at home in a place of worship than to make me rigidly follow their preference.

The period of adolescence can be very tricky for parents and teens when it comes to faith. Theoretically, teens no longer have to go to church with you because they can be left safely at home alone; so how do you encourage kids to still participate in a church community? When they're in high school, consider their preferences. The hope is that by the time they're teenagers, they have developed a community of friends within the church you attend and still enjoy going. If that is not the case, it's important for them to plug in somewhere else they feel comfortable. Let them visit three or four kinds of places if they want, or allow them to attend a friend's place of worship as I did. It changed everything for me. And I'm so thankful my parents allowed it.

Other things can help foster the faith relationships at older ages, even if a teen has never been to church. Plenty of nondenominational churches out there want to spark a fire for people seeking "more." These places are noninvasive and inviting, even intriguing. I've also found that kids enjoy church activities more when they're focused on helping the community and helping others. For years, kids have been told that they're too young to help out and make a difference, but when they enter middle school, they're old enough to take on some responsibilities. Plus, middle schoolers are in that sweet spot when they don't have jobs, can't drive, and don't have any money, and they often feel like they are helpless to combat the injustices of this world. So, when there's an opportunity to help the homeless, help migrants, or help collect toys for underprivileged kids at Christmas, this empowers children with knowledge that they can make a difference.

Another benefit to being part of a faith-based community is that while kids are learning lessons about faith, they're also learning how to deal with people in their group who they may not necessarily have anything in common with. They must build relationships with other people at church, even when it's hard. Often, when a kid faces a situation at school with another child who aggravates them, avoidance might be the best way around the issue. But in a faith-based community, it's a little different. You're both working together toward a goal and have an "other-centric" posture. For Christians, the focus is on serving God and having Him work through you to help others. That translates into tolerance, which helps you grow as a person. Tolerance helps in athletics and in academic achievement. It also helps when it comes to personality, as you're not self-focused. Instead, you're centered on being the best you can be and helping lead others in a direction that's positive.

I've known Scott for about seven and a half years, and have gotten to learn from him as well as hang out with him. Scott was always there to give advice, comfort, or tools to use to get things done. He always tells me the truth, even when it's a hard topic or something that I don't necessarily want to hear. He helped me start a leadership Bible study with friends from my old school. It was something I was nervous about, as well as excited to do. Throughout, he helped me to gain the courage to ask my friends to join and participate, even though I had doubts that they would not want to. It turned out to be one of the best decisions I have made, because it brought me closer to my friends as well as God through my faith. It also helped me to surround myself with people that had similar goals and morals. He helped guide our group through tough decisions that we would face throughout high school and with our friend groups. Scott showed us how to be real friends to each other and others, and to lead by example in everyday life.

One of my main takeaways from my relationship with Scott was learning how to forgive through many different circumstances. I learned through him having to forgive me, as well as him leading me through forgiving people I thought I would never forgive. This relationship has molded me into the man I am today and will be in the future. He has showed me to never stop growing in your faith and character, and that is something I will hold close to me as I grow older and face new challenges in life.

—Charlie

Belonging to a faith-based community also exposes our children to leaders with moral integrity. Enough leaders in our society are leading people in the wrong direction. Many times, the wrong direction has a lot to do with social climbing or doing what's cool or attention-getting. A teen might be hungry for attention and use their gift of leadership in the wrong way. It takes courage and conviction to lead with high character and integrity.

Many teens are hungry for a great leader who inspires them to grow in a positive direction. They desire one who builds others up instead of leading them into a dark place.

Some of my first memories of Scott are from this Little League team and the positive and energetic spirit he always had. Despite a sub-par record that in no way reflected the potential of our team, you could always count on Scott leading us to have the best time of any team on the diamond. Little did I know at the time that this relationship would foster into one of the most integral and lasting friendships of my life.

I was able to breeze through elementary and middle school as one of the more popular and happy kids around with incredible potential for a successful future. All the while I kept in contact with Scott mostly through the youth group at Peachtree Road United Methodist Church and my friendship with his son. At this point in my life, I saw Scott more as a parent figure and mentor rather than a close friend. In high school, I became consumed with the ideas of popularity, partying, and girls. I was still achieving my goals in the classroom and in sports, and I walked around the halls with a smile on my face; however, not everything outside of school was going as well as I let on. I began running with the wrong crowd on the weekends and during the summer, and we were more concerned with where the next party was than anything else. It was the relentless idea that drinking and hanging with the "cool crowd" would make me popular and, ultimately, happy that led to the rough relationship I experienced with my father and a few unfortunate run-ins with the law along the way. I didn't always feel like I could talk to my dad when problems arose and just saw him as the hypocritical entity that had me grounded for what seemed like the majority of high school. Rarely could we have a serious conversation without one of us turning it into a screaming match. Therefore, when problems came up, I tended to just internalize them and never really vocalized my emotions. This led me to make situations worse for myself and I began turning to unhealthy outlets for release.

Scott Whitehead was the one person I knew I could turn to who would never judge me but rather in all ways be a pillar of support, and no matter what was going on in his busy schedule, I knew he would always be able to pencil me in. I started to see Scott as more of a true friend to whom I could disclose everything emotionally that I was experiencing in my life. At first, I was hesitant to disclose some details of information to Scott and even made situations out to not be as bad as they were, and I knew that he could see through the BS I would sling across the breakfast table. However, he was patient and determined to help me open up and be there to help develop me into the young man I had all the potential to be. He told me that in the timeline of our entire lives these setbacks are only tiny little blips on the spectrum and that there is always so much to look forward to. With my trust in him and his leadership, I was able to get back and remain on track in my life. I graduated from high school with honors, had a better relationship with my parents, and was surrounded by good people that helped to project me in the right direction. All was going well in my life, and I was ready to take on the next chapter of my life at the University of Georgia and I could not have been happier.

But after an incident with a fraternity my freshman year, I became deeply depressed. Scott reminded me to remain faithful and trust in God's plan for me, which isn't always the easiest thing to do and is often forgotten in the college setting. We also discussed the importance in only surrounding yourself with good people that truly care for you, because these are the people that will long remain relevant in your life and help support and drive you to achieving your goals and full potential in life.

—Cameron

Kids look up to the leaders within faith-based organizations, but they also look up to you, their parent or mentor. For that reason, it's important for parents and mentors to model being a person of faith every day of the week, not just on worship day. You must show leadership—do unto others as you would have others do unto you. Think about how to be a better person by volunteering and using your gifts to help others. Practice your faith at home. Take on volunteer or leadership roles within your church. All of this is important because children can see right through hypocrisy. They see fathers who dress up for church on Sunday but stay out late drinking and carousing on other nights of the week, ignoring their responsibilities at home and acting selfishly, and they don't respect that. In fact, they resent it. Why, later in life, would they seek advice or help from someone who never lived as they preached, or who expected their child to do one thing while they did another?

Truett Cathy, the founder of Chick-fil-A, had great character and faith. A humble man, he never moved out of the modest ranch house that he started out in, even though he ran a privately owned five-billion-dollar company. He emphasized to me the importance of a father's participation in a child's life. He once told me, "Scott, when it comes to faith-based and youth organization attendance, in a family where a mother and father come to church, there's an 85 to 90 percent chance the kid will come to church. When it's the mother only who brings the child, the chances that the child will come drops to 40 to 50 percent. When it's the father only, it jumps back up to 70 to 75 percent." A father's influence is huge.

When a parent and a child are in a community of faith together, they're growing in their faith alongside each other and have a common interest in serving others. When you get into setting expectations for kids, which is one of our other pillars, you've created a base for a child to understand that there's something bigger than them in the family and bigger than this world.

Growth Opportunities Through Mission Trips

Mission trips can have a big impact on a teen's faith journey. Typically, parents do not go along on youth mission trips, so they don't often get to witness the growth and development of their teen's character over the course of the week. So many times, I have wished a parent could be a fly on the wall to proudly witness their son or daughter serving someone in need. I've had the great privilege and honor to go on many of these trips and experience my young friends' immersion in being about others. Mission trips can truly be a pivotal moment for many kids at a very important time in their lives.

I believe that as a parent, it's important to work on your faith alongside your children. Go on faith-based family mission trips, if possible, as they are a great way for everyone to grow in relationships while participating in an "other-centric" world.

What happens when you run up against resistance? What if your teenager doesn't want to do these things with their parents? Try this tactic that I used on one of our mission trips, when quite a few kids were complaining about bugs or their sleeping quarters.

I had relationships and credibility with the kids, so I said, "You knew what the experience would be like. Why did you sign up?"

"Well, my mom made me come."

"Okay, your mom made you come, but think about this—wouldn't you rather have a little bit of self-growth and realize how blessed you are to have everything you have, or would you rather just be in this funk and complain? I want you to think about it. I want you to look around, and I want you to remember why the majority of the adults are here. It's about helping you guys be in a relationship with Christ and see what they've been blessed to see and what's guiding them in their lives. Think about that and circle back to me in a couple of days."

With about 90 percent of the kids, that kind of conversation helps them get in the groove. You're not doing them any service as a mentor/adult if you're not pointing something out to them. They need help understanding and processing. It's your job to ask good questions and make them think differently about things.

In my experience, there's no better way to foster faith growth than on a mission trip or a retreat where you spend an entire week helping others. Often, at the end of the week, someone you've been serving breaks down crying because they had no expectation in life of anyone doing anything for them. They may be disabled, elderly, or down on their luck. And you get to watch your kids experience the realization that they've impacted someone else and understand how good that feels.

Later, when I talk about it with them, I say, "I saw your faces when Miss Ella told her story; you could have heard a pin drop in that aisle. That feeling is what God wants us to have all the time—and that's about others."

Pointing out those moments can be helpful to teens because it plants a seed in them about the importance of finding moments to be about others and not about themselves. It might only be a fleeting realization—after all, they're just kids. But the seed has been planted, and it grows, and the kids become hungry for more. Later in life, they can pull back and remember when they experienced "a natural feeling, a calm feeling." They'll want to capture that feeling again, and they'll start digging to find it.

CHAPTER 5

Expectations

The concept of expectations is a little tricky to understand. It doesn't mean setting expectations for your son or daughter so that they will follow in your footsteps to become a doctor or a lawyer, go to your alma mater, or win the state championship so you can relive your moments of glory.

Expectations are about embracing your child's God-given gifts and helping them grow into those gifts.

Setting expectations teaches kids early on that their life's trajectory is based on their own decisions. It gives them a measure of self-control and is one of the biggest and best things you can do for your child. You're putting the responsibility for how their life plays out on them, which is where it belongs; you're simply the support system. This means they are not following some sort of predetermined path set out for them by previous generations.

Instead, they should put serious thought into who they want to be, where they want to go, and what's their life purpose will be. Being held accountable by expectations motivates kids to make good decisions.

We'll look more at helping kids discover their gifts a little later in this chapter, but first, let's focus on how to communicate with your child about expectations.

The Message on Expectations Kids Need to Hear

Integrity is doing the right thing, even if it hurts you.

Setting expectations for your kids means you need to be clear with them on three things.

1. You expect them to do the right thing, in any given situation.
2. You provide 100 percent support, without micromanaging and looking over their shoulder every step of the way.
3. They set their goals, not you.

Finding Their Own Path

As much as we like to think that our children are adorable copies of us who will enjoy the same things that we enjoy and excel in the ways we excel, they are clearly not. This becomes evident the moment they learn the word, "No!" "No," they don't want to play soccer. "No," they don't want to go to that concert with you. "No," they don't want you to read your favorite book to them. And "No," they definitely will not eat pasta with tomato sauce. "It's got onions in it!"

Embrace their unique tastes, desires for the future, and skill sets. Give them opportunities to discover what they like and don't like. A dad who has dreamed of having a son who plays football and becomes the star quarterback might be initially disappointed when his son has no interest in sports. That father's duty as a parent is to find out what his child's gifts are. His son might lean more toward engineering, coding, cooking, music, or writing. Sometimes a child will immediately gravitate toward an activity, or sometimes a person or scenario pushes them into an opportunity to try something you never imagined. Be reasonable: Don't overschedule them with Tae Kwon Do on Mondays, guitar lessons on Tuesdays, tennis on Wednesdays, T-ball on Thursdays, and soccer on Saturdays. Allow them time to daydream, explore, be in nature, and play with their friends. In this way, they'll come to know themselves.

It's difficult for parents to follow all three steps outlined above because we all like to control people, especially our own children. It's an easy habit to fall into. You start out being overprotective of them when they're infants and toddlers because they don't understand basic concepts like danger. So you keep them away from the stove, put up baby gates near the stairs, and hold their hand while walking in parking lots. Over time, as they learn not to run into traffic, know to get on the right school bus, and remember to call you if they want to go to Billy's house, you start communicating your expectations for their behavior. Then you can take a step back.

As children grow, the list of things they can do by themselves expands, and they realize you are there to support them and catch them if they fall. They realize that they have a safety net in you—not to bail them out, but to talk them through what's bothering them. You're still a disciplinarian and a parent who has set up guardrails. If children choose to go down the wrong path, you need to talk to them about that decision—was it because they were trying to be accepted, trying to learn, or wanting to take risks? Listen thoughtfully as your son or daughter talks this through with you. Then, summarize what they said to make sure you heard them correctly and show them that there are better ways to learn and grow stronger in healthy instead of destructive ways. Reiterate that you almost never learn from success; the real lessons come from mistakes.

Our parents told us all the time growing up, "You're a Whitehead and don't ever forget it." It's such a simple statement, but it made us proud of who we are and the name we were born with. It made us feel like we were an unbreakable tribe that could take on anything. That did two important things for me. First, it made me have the security to know I always can come back to the people I love, and they will be there for me. This allowed me to take chances and have a safety net to fall back into. Second, it taught me that life isn't always about just me. It made me care even more for the people closest to me because they cared so much for me and made it known.

—P. Whitehead

When I was a small and curious third grader, I learned an important and embarrassing lesson. I was looking at the bright-red fire alarm lever in my classroom, wondering what would happen if I pulled it. In THIRD grade! My desire to find out got the best of me, and I reached right up and pulled that lever. Chaos erupted in that school. Students, teachers, and administrators spilled into the hallways and out into the schoolyard. Firefighters showed up to investigate, and worst of all, I was caught, red-handed. My parents were called, and I got a lecture from both them and the principal.

But I learned an important lesson that day. There's a time to be curious and explore, but sometimes, curiosity is obnoxious and disruptive and shows up in the wrong way at the wrong time. My mom and dad quickly handed me a new set of expectations and helped me see that my impulsive act had wasted time, money, and resources.

Needless to say, I never had the urge to pull a fire alarm again.

The way kids break their parents' expectations can take many forms. Let's say instead of setting off the fire alarm, the principal calls to tell you your son hit another boy. You wonder, *Why was he not able to deal with his feelings without resorting to violence?* Once you bring your child home, he is crying and angry and upset, while you are trying to control your own anger. You're mad at him for getting in trouble, but you need to set that aside to get to the root of the problem.

Kids need help in knowing how to deal with their impulses and anger, among many other emotions.

Parents and mentors have learned over the years how to deal with adversity, how to deal with bullies who pick on them, and how to handle tense situations without resorting to violence. It's up to us to share our knowledge so that our children don't get into trouble. They can't be bubble-wrapped to protect them from life's slings and arrows, but they can be thoughtfully advised and guided.

For the parents of the boy who got in a fight, two approaches could be taken. There's the expectations talk, and then there's the controlling talk.

In the "controlling" version of the talk, the parent yells, "Go to your room. I am so embarrassed by you! I cannot believe you did that. You are not my son. I don't know where you came from. You will not do this again!" Those kinds of comments tear down a child's ego instead of building it up. This is a volatile moment when your kid feels like he's let himself down. Other phrases that tear down a child: "You were horrible, stupid, incompetent, an embarrassment to the family!" Words like that can rip apart the parent-child relationship being formed during adolescence, because the child doesn't feel like the parent has any faith in him or respect for him, and he may have very little respect for himself. That kind of fractured relationship may undermine the ability of the parents and mentor to have any control of that kid as he gets older, and rebellion may result.

Using your own anger does not help solve the underlying issue. That angry boy doesn't know how to control himself. Your role is to teach him how, without further fueling the fire or undermining your relationship of trust and support.

If you've got a good relationship with your child, use this time for an "expectations" talk. Ask what's been going on at school and if he's feeling anxious or stressed out about anything. Try to approach the situation by offering some solutions and positive ways for dealing with it. Ask, "Why do you feel you did that? I know you're extremely smart and you knew it was wrong. I don't have to tell you that."

Convey this message to your child: "You're a part of something that's bigger than just you. Keep being humble. Some amazing things will happen when you take the focus off you and put it on others. Trust me on this. I know it's hard to see right now, but it will happen." A sense of responsibility will grow out of representing a family's name. This is similar to their career life, when they will represent their family, friends, and companies. All making them a part of something bigger than themselves.

The summer after my junior year I interned for Scott at Chateau Energy Solutions. There I was lucky to meet a group of the highest quality human beings. Pam became my "office mom" and kept me busy throughout the summer. And with Scott, I saw what being a boss truly means, which is not just developing your employees to achieve the greatest possible profits, but more importantly, to develop your employees to be the greatest possible community leaders and Christians they can be.

I was lucky enough to work as an intern again the spring semester of my senior year. At that point, I was doing some things in my life I wasn't proud of and got arrested and taken to the DeKalb County jail. I was so worried it would jeopardize my internship. But instead of reprimanding me, Scott shared some of his own experiences from when he was a teenager. Our relationship grew beyond that of boss/employee, and even more than mentor-mentee. After opening up to me, Scott became one of my best friends on the planet.

I appreciate so much all that Scott has given me. He gave me exposure to a company culture that I instill in my family relationships, my friendships, my partnerships, and hopefully one day my own company. But it's so much more than that. The conversations and experiences I've had with him had an immeasurable impact on me as a person and in turn on the community I'm a part of.

—Michael

When you're growing into a young adult, you're really just trying to hold it together while making friends, doing your homework, getting good grades, and figuring out who you are. So much input comes at you day and night from parents, teachers, friends, coaches, and neighbors. Even strangers ask, "What do you want to do when you grow up?" Kids realize there's an unspoken expectation that they have the privilege—regardless of whether they are rich or poor—of getting to choose who they will be on this earth. The expectation is that they should do the best they can with what they have. If they are not doing their best with their time here to better themselves and to better the lives of others, then they are really missing opportunities for a happy and fulfilling life.

You are practicing for who you want to be.

What Happens When Your Kid Doesn't Meet Expectations?

Two teens get invited to a party. Both teenagers and their parents know that drinking happens at high school parties. The question is, what do you do about it?

Parents who use a controlling, carrot-and-stick method of parenting would forbid their child from going to such a party. This, however, is the wrong approach because it takes away the child's ability to practice decision-making skills, which are especially important when situations aren't black and white. Having someone over your shoulder saying, "Don't do that, don't do this," probably makes a huge negative impact and develops the kid into someone who always makes decisions based on what a spouse or parent thinks, rather than making decisions based on the expectations they have set for themselves.

Parents who set expectations for a child to always do what is best for their lives and that of others leads to a different outcome. For example, your daughter knows she's a part of your family, in which it is clear there are some things you do and don't do. She has earned her privileges and a degree of autonomy. If she is disrespectful, you don't let her do whatever she wants whenever she wants. Yes, she might make a mistake and drink alcohol, and, yes, she might not meet her own expectations. However, when the boundaries are clearly laid out, the auto-correct that you've built into her kicks in. She might choose to go to that party, and she might even have a beer, but when she realizes the party's getting out of hand, she has the strength to make good decisions. She stops drinking because she knows it limits her abilities to make good choices and live up to her obligations and expectations. She asks for a ride home from somebody who hasn't had any alcohol.

The same applies to a kid at college who decides to go to a party one night instead of studying. He drinks too much and misses class the next day because he's suffering from a hangover. If he's been trained well in the expectations of what is necessary to be successful in his chosen field, he will realize what that night of drinking has cost him; it's not meshing with the future life he has planned. He rethinks how he will behave in the future.

It's important to learn from your mistakes. Yes, we want to protect our children from making mistakes in the first place, but it's hard for them to learn if they never get to try.

When parents set expectations, they can feel comfortable that even when kids make mistakes, they're able to learn from them and reset their course. When parents do the opposite and make decisions for their child, the message it sends is, "I don't trust you with your own life." Those are the kids who will go to the party and think, *Hmmm. How much can I get away with here?* If they're never allowed to get away with anything, then going to a party or any act of rebellion is a way to escape that parental control and find their own freedom. Most parents don't want that outcome.

My parents were forgiving when we made mistakes. As we got older, they started to loosen the rope upon us as we earned respect from them. My mom and I got into small arguments in the kitchen, because they would not let me go to a party, friend's house, etc. There was never a point when she just said "no" without a reason. She always gave a reason. As the rope would go out, I would make a mistake and the rope would get pulled in a little. My parents always gave us the chance to earn that freedom back. When we messed up, we would sit down and have a conversation about what happened and how to gain that freedom we had before.

—P. Whitehead

Expect to Fail

It's important for parents to set good expectations, help direct kids on a course to success, and support them as they get there. But it's also crucial for parents and mentors to help kids understand that failure is a part of life. Trying and failing only helps us grow and become stronger human beings.

Recently, I held my final Bible study with a group of young men who were going to the University of Georgia and the University of South Carolina.

"Guys, you're going to fail," I told them. "And when that happens, you're going to feel like you're on your own, but in reality, you're not alone. Your parents, me, and a group of other people in your world have supported you all these years and we're still there for you, even if we're not there in person. You know our expectations for you, and you've got to live up to that. I make decisions every single day, and I can't make them for everyone else, including y'all, as much as I would sometimes like to. Your success is literally up to you, and you've got to set your expectations that will shape your future. When you do fail, the next day when you're not feeling so good, pick up the phone and call and let's talk through it. Or alternatively, just push the "reset" button—realize what you did was not helping you get where you need to be.

"Conversely, when you do really good stuff—you get leadership positions or great grades, for example—realize that's 100 percent due to the expectations that created that drive and effort. All of it was self-realized, but remember how we've talked about fulfilling your natural gifts and how important that is."

Expectations Around Dating

Having clear expectations for your child's behavior includes a subject that often makes parents uncomfortable: dating. It's hard to think of your child growing up and having more mature relationships with people outside the family, especially romantic relationships.

But if you've built a good relationship that has a strong foundation of faith and clear expectations, your child will more than likely make good decisions.

Often, your child will develop relationships outside the family with people who are similar to them, as an individual's personality and tendencies are an average of the five people they hang out with. They are likely to seek out other kids who are grounded in faith and have strong relationships with their parents. For instance, a child with a strong parental relationship does not enjoy going to the home of a friend who does not have a good relationship with a parent. It might not feel right in their inner compass. A child who has been raised with internal expectations of what they're going to do with their life, and who knows the things they need to do to accomplish their goals, will confidently follow those expectations. They also do not want to disappoint those they hold in high regard and want to model themselves after those types of people.

Children with a good set of internal expectations tend not to choose to hang out with the fast crowd. They've seen the drama that moving too fast can create.

Decision-Making

As a businessperson, I often use examples from my work to help parents. For instance, employees used to want to come into my office and tell me everything that they were doing.

"What do you want me to do about this issue?" an employee would ask.

I would answer them with a blank stare. "This is your customer, your territory," I would finally say. "You know best. If I had to jump in and figure out the situation on this account, then why do I need you to do this job?"

How does that relate to parenting? Your child knows his social scene, his academic life, his athletic gifts, and his goals better than you do. When your child asks you a question, don't give him the answer! Instead, help walk him through the decision-making process.

Share stories around how you made decisions and discuss whether your choices brought you good things or failure. "When I was your age, it would have taken me two days or a week to make that decision," you might tell them.

When I coach leadership skills, I say the goal is to fail fast. If you must make a decision, you should think about it and pray about it if you're a person of faith. Once you have a gut feeling about a decision, analysis paralysis might set in, and you may then begin to wonder, *What will people think?* When you fail fast, you learn every time you fail, and won't fail the same way twice. Make the decision. If it's wrong, you've just learned something, and no matter what anyone else thinks, it's important for you. You keep growing and moving forward, and it keeps getting easier as we move along. No one likes to fail at the beginning. We're taught to avoid failing. But I couldn't do half of what I do now if I hadn't failed as a teenager.

There are country songs galore about people like me!

A big difference exists between unintentional failure and intentional failure. Intentional failure is when you start doing something with the full or partial understanding that it will not add to your future or support your life goals. That kind of intentional failure is not acceptable, and kids should know and understand that.

Unintentional failure, on the other hand, results from trying something. In many instances, teens need to put themselves out there and try new things, like start a new job, ask a guy or a girl out on a date for the first time, or step outside their comfort zone and try a challenging class in a new subject. All those things are ways kids grow socially, academically, or financially. Those attempts and tries are linked directly to their success, and every single time they fail, they learn something.

Sometimes you create success, sometimes it's a colossal failure, and sometimes it's a little bit of both. Any scenario is fine, because through failure, you discover that perhaps something is not your style of learning, or it's not a good business idea because no one wants to buy your product, or it's not a good way to approach a dating or friend situation, even though you thought the opposite. You won't repeat the same action after you realize how it didn't work for you. You go back in and approach the situation differently, with more perspective, experience, and wisdom. While you may not have 100 percent success the next time, the outcome will be better than before.

Intentional failure involves handling things in a way that are detrimental to your reputation or health. You put yourself in jeopardy with thoughts like, I'm going out and I'm going to get drunk tonight, or I'm going to get in a fight, or I'm going to drive fast because I want an adrenaline rush.

Unintentional failure involves stepping out of your comfort zone and choosing things that align with the expectations you, your parents, and the community have instilled in you. Unintentional failure should be cherished. Failure is one of the best friends that we've got, because there's no better teacher. We can't learn anything being right all the time.

Future Expectations

I never told my kids that they had to go to college. Instead, I wanted them to set their own expectations for what they wanted to do with their lives. I did, however, talk about the subject with my wife quite often, and the children heard these conversations. We talked openly about the importance of college, the great people we met while there, and the fun times we'd had, along with the amazing classes we took and the professors we learned from. We also talked about what happened to kids we knew who didn't go to college. Over time, our children absorbed the importance of a college education.

When I went to college, my parents generously covered my tuition. As I got older, I realized that perhaps as a result, I didn't take it as seriously as I should have. I did work hard, but I likely would have worked harder if I'd felt fully invested in it.

Soon enough, our children got to the age where grades and other factors started to really count. When my son was in eighth grade, I told him, "If you go to college, I'm not paying for it."

"What do you mean? You can't afford it?"

"No, that's not a problem at all. But when I went to school, my dad paid for it all, and I took it for granted. I had no sweat equity in the game. I'm not going to do that to you. I want you to really value your education."

"Well, yeah, I want to go to college!"

I wanted my children to know that they shouldn't take out student loans, so they needed to figure out how to pay for school through other means. Thereafter, both my kids knew that they needed to find a way to pay for college themselves. I wanted them to grow excited about their futures and want to invest in themselves.

My kids' goal in high school wasn't just to graduate, it was to excel in all areas—academics, sports, leadership, volunteering. They needed options because they didn't know which activity would be their ticket. Being involved with a team sport, as a band member, or on a leadership committee is an invaluable experience that helps grow time-management skills and leadership. Each arena teaches you what's effective leadership and what is not, and you learn how to pour whatever talents you have into the greater good. Having the goal of finding a way to pay for college was just another vehicle that we used as parents so that our kids would have a vested interest.

For my son, a Hunt leadership scholarship paid for SMU; only twenty-five of those scholarships were given out of eight hundred applicants. My daughter's 4.3 grade point average and a high score on her standardized testing got her an academic scholarship to the University of Georgia. This helped set them up for graduating from college without the heavy burden of debt, and it gave them an enormous amount of pride that their own successes had led them to that place.

During the college decision process, I felt overwhelmed because I had never made such a big decision in my life. My dad went to the University of Alabama, and if you know him, it is obvious. I knew I wanted to go to the University of Georgia, but I felt that choosing Georgia would be frowned upon because we had been Alabama fans my entire life. One morning at breakfast, my dad started talking about my college decision process and mentioned that he would always support me whether I went to Alabama or not. He knew I was deciding between Georgia and Alabama at the time and told me that he did not care what college I went to, so long as I was happy with my decision and was making the decision for myself. He told me about his college process and said my decisions did not need to cater to other people's needs so long as I was happy. I thought about this for a couple of days and finally decided to go to Georgia. My mom and dad have been nothing but supportive and happy for me, but if they had not reassured me that I was not going to disappoint him or told me how he related to my situation, I might have made a decision that was not right for me.

—A. Whitehead

They're on their own now—one is still in college and one has graduated—making their own decisions, but they know that they're always welcome home with open arms if they ever need to regroup. I tell my children all the time how proud I am of how many of their own goals they've achieved.

When you put solid guardrails and safety nets in place for your children, they know that taking the big swings to achieve their goals may result in occasional failures, but they'll be able to take care of themselves and find deep satisfaction with what they do in life.

They will not be able to succeed and fulfill their destiny if they don't feel like they have a place of refuge or support system at home, or if they don't feel responsible for their own successes. Let them know, continually, that you are confident in their abilities to succeed but that you have their backs should they need you.

Just make sure children know that they have a safe place to return to when they need to regroup, recharge, and try again.

CHAPTER 6

Time

One common thread runs through every topic discussed in this book: time. Spending time with your child transcends everything. It fills up their bucket, so to speak. Spending time with a child shows that you love them, helps build their confidence, and puts you well on the way to nurturing a solid citizen for the future. It's a given that building a relationship, providing support, and doing any of the things we've talked about in this book thus far requires that you spend time with your children. Time together helps build the relationship, but it results in so much more than that. It's about modeling and building patterns for them that they will incorporate in their own lives and in how they treat other people. It gives kids the confidence to feel comfortable and fulfilled to not only learn and grow for themselves but also to reach out and help others.

What do I mean when I say spend time with your kids? I don't mean sitting next to them on the couch while you're both looking at your phones.

Spending time means taking an active role in their lives, engaging with them, and taking time to have meaningful conversations. In short, it means just being there.

Making Time in Every Stage

Spending time with your kids starts in infancy and continues throughout their lives. The way you spend time might change over time, but the importance never wavers.

Infancy. It's important to spend time with children from the moment they're born. Talking to your baby, interacting with her, and holding her helps the two of you bond and builds her sense of comfort and security from the very beginning of life. At this stage, spending time with your child mostly involves simply caring for them. It includes changing diapers, bathing them, feeding them, putting them to bed—all times when you can talk to your baby, make eye contact, shower them with your touch, and help them know they are loved.

Preschool and Elementary Years. Once your child starts walking, they gain a little independence. Your role as a parent includes that of caregiver, but you're much more now. Take time with your children at this stage to be an active part of their lives both at home and in their activities. In the preschool years, you're still helping get them ready for the day, and at night you're still directing bath time and reading bedtime stories. Get down on the floor and play blocks, put things together, play pretend. As they grow, if they're already interested in sports, volunteer to coach their T-ball or run-and-kick soccer teams. Take them to school or to dance class and enjoy your time together in the car on the way to and from lessons.

For school-aged children, volunteering is a great way to spend time with your kids and at the same time become part of their community. Volunteer to teach their Sunday school class, sign up to chaperone field trips, take cupcakes to their class on their birthday, or volunteer in their classroom. By being part of their world, you show your kids that you want to be involved in their lives. They also see your interactions with their teachers and with other students. It gives them a sense of pride and helps them understand that they're a part of something bigger than them.

This is when spending time with your kids is easy, because they want to spend time with you. How many times have you come home from work and had your kids run out to greet you, tug on your pants leg, and say, "Dad, let's go throw the ball"? Take advantage of this enthusiasm and spend time with them. Time together is particularly impactful at this time in their lives, for two reasons.

First, you're modeling behavior, and kids are like sponges—they soak it all up. They're watching what you do and how you act. When they see you volunteer in their classroom, they not only know you care enough about them to be involved at their school, but they see it's important to give back to their community. When you come home from work and play catch before supper, they know they're an important part of your life. On the other hand, if you come home from work frustrated and tell them to leave you alone because you had a bad day and go off by yourself, you're showing your kids that work is horrible.

Your actions speak to them, and you're constantly modeling for them.

Second, when you make a point to spend time with your kids when they're young, they will still want you involved in their lives when they're teenagers. It's all about plugging into their lives. One way I recommend doing this is to "get ahead" of your kids. Volunteer at church to help with the youth group when your kids are still young. Your kids will grow up watching you interact with older kids, and at the same time, you'll learn and grow by figuring out how to get along with older kids before you have to do it with your own. When your kids reach their teen years and are in youth group and hanging out with friends, you're there too, and it hopefully should not seem intrusive or embarrassing to your kids since you've been involved with the youth group since they were little.

Teenagers. If you've set the foundation and plugged in ahead of time, your kids are comfortable having you around when they're teenagers. The time you spend together might look a little different than when they were younger, but you're still there for them, and as an accepted member of their community, you have their confidence.

Being around, even if you're just like a fly on the wall, is a great position to be in from a parent's perspective, and sometimes it happens without any planning or intention. One time when I was at a youth retreat, I saw a girl sitting all alone on the steps. I went over and sat beside her, and we started having a conversation. Eventually, a few other kids gathered around, and then a few more, until eventually, about thirty kids were gathered around talking. I was no longer the leader in this conversation; the group had taken on a life of its own. But everyone was interacting with each other and seemed comfortable talking, even with their adult leader (me) still in their midst.

My point is that sometimes kids will become so comfortable around you that they'll talk about subjects that make you want to raise a flag and say, "Hello, do you see me sitting right here?" I think every parent has experienced this at some point. Often, it happens in the car, when you're driving and the kids are in the back seat, and they're talking like they're in a limo with a privacy window between the driver and the passenger seat. In reality, you can hear everything they're saying. It's a comfort level that you've built up in your relationship with your kids, and that's a great position to be in as a parent. You'll hear conversations between your kids and their friends and be able to learn what they're focused on and what they're worried about. You won't be privy to everything going on in your teen's life, but you'll have a good gut feeling about them and where things stand for them.

In the teen years, being part of your child's community and

gaining a comfort level with them is important, but also remember that it is still imperative to spend time with them one-on-one. Get on their turf and participate in things that they enjoy doing. Find things you enjoy doing together. Maybe you both like running and can train for a 5K. Attend their games, even if it's not one of your favorite sports. Showing up at their activities means a lot because they know you're busy and need to work it in to your schedule, so even in these years when they might not want to sit right next to you, they'll still appreciate that you came.

Remember, time in these years often must be on the young person's own terms to some extent, otherwise you wind up dealing with a sulky teenager.

When I was a teen, my dad had the grand idea that we were going to build a car together. He loved mechanics and engineering, and working on cars, boats, or anything with an engine was his idea of fun. It wasn't my idea of fun. I said I didn't want to build a car, but he didn't give me an option.

One day, a VW Beetle showed up at our house.

"Dad, what's this?" I asked.

"That's what we're going to use for the chassis to build your car."

"I told you I don't want to build a car," I said.

"You'll have fun. We're building a car."

A little later, an eighteen-wheeler showed up in our driveway and delivered a crate to our front yard. It was the kit for the car. Then, one Saturday morning, Dad woke me up at 8:00 a.m., after I'd been out late the night before playing in a high school football game.

"We're going to build a car," Dad said. I grudgingly went downstairs to the garage. All the time, I felt like he was doing the work for him, not for me.

Don't get me wrong, my dad was great at spending time with us. We spent weekends on the lake in our boat and played catch in the yard. But I'm using the car as an example to show that sometimes, when your kids are teenagers, it's more important to find things they like to do rather than make them do the things you want to do.

You might have no interest at all in gaming, but watch what happens if you go up to your kid one day and say, "Hey, want to show me how to play that game?" Your sullen teenager's face will light up because you want to spend time with him.

Throughout their childhood. Many things you do to spend time with your kids won't necessarily change with their life stage. In fact, starting family traditions when kids are young is a great way to ensure that those traditions continue through the years, even into adulthood.

- Family dinners. Finding time to enjoy a meal together might seem like a luxury with the busy lives many families lead. But research has shown that parents who make a point to sit down and eat with their kids on a regular basis raise children who perform better academically, are less likely to get in trouble, and have lower rates of obesity and lower risk of depression. It doesn't have to be every night. Aim for at least two to three nights a week to start. Mealtimes are the perfect time to have conversations and learn what's going on in each other's lives.

- Special getaways. I found when raising my kids that our lake house was a great way to spend time with the family. You're away from other distractions, commitments, and responsibilities, and you really have time to focus on being with each other. Your kids are sort of being held captive without feeling like they're being held captive. Your getaway spot doesn't have to be a second home—it can just be a special place you all like to go. Maybe you enjoy camping, or perhaps you have a beach condo that you rent each year for your summer vacation.
- Institute family night. Just as it's important for married couples to have a date night, I also like to include a family night once a week. Set aside time to put away your smartphones and hang out with each other. You can play board games, watch a movie, or go out and do something fun like bowling or roller skating.

Finding Time in Your Busy Life

It baffles me when I hear parents say, "I wish I could do more with my kids, but I just don't have the time." I know we're all busy, but once you decide to have children, or if you have children already, they should be your priority. It's never too late to make time for your kids, but it is more difficult to change your habits the later you start.

On a positive note, I've noticed that fathers have gotten better at spending time with their kids over the past couple of generations. I think parenting styles in the 1950s and 1960s were influenced by the Great Depression. It made the generation that lived through it and the generation that followed fearful about making a living and providing for their families. They never wanted to go back to those times, so the generations learned from one another to value a strong work ethic. A good work ethic is great, but you must also have balance.

The most important thing that my parents did for us was being present. Looking back, I could not be more thankful for how much time our parents spent with us. They never missed a baseball game, football game, church every Sunday, my sister's dance recitals … everything and anything we did, they were there. It made us feel loved and supported. When Dad would go on business meetings to cool places, if we were available, he would take us with him. Spending time with each other and seeing that we all cared about each other made us grow closer.

The things I have mentioned above made me love and respect my parents. I wanted them to know that I was listening to them by following their expectations. It meant the world to me when that was recognized, and they gave me more freedom as I got older. I would go two steps forward and one back, but that is all about the learning process. Living those mistakes and learning from them with parents who cared made all the difference.

—P. Whitehead

If you're a mother or father with a career that takes you away from home and you're reading this book to find out how to spend more time with your children, I recommend that you start incrementally. Allocate two more hours a week with your kids than

God calls all of us to work to support our families financially, but God also wants us to be there for our children.

what you're spending now and try that for a month. If you can do two, then I'm sure you can do four. Each month, build on the amount of time. My guess is we can all find two hours, especially in an entire week, where we can show up and be with our kids.

Do it, and your child will notice. You might get the question, "Dad, what are you doing here?" Tell them they are your priority in your life, and even though you have to work to support the family, you want them to know that they are important to you. Your kids might not tell you they appreciate the time you're spending with them, but you'll be able to see a difference in their attitudes and behavior.

It's easier now more than ever to stay connected with your kids, even on days you work late or have to travel. Set a time to Facetime with them, or text your kids to ask how their day was. When you're on the road, pick up something special to bring home that lets them know you were thinking of them even while away.

I would never have expected to one day call Scott one of my best friends. Until, one day, I reached out to see if he wanted to grab some lunch. After catching up for a good hour, I felt like God had called him back into my life for not only support, but guidance on how to refine myself as the best person I could be.

Throughout Scott mentoring me, I have come to learn many things that help me go through my day being appreciative of all the blessings that have presented themselves to me. As I was dealing with parental conflicts at home, I was not mature enough to realize that my parents were great people and just looking out for the best for me. Instead, as a fifteen-year-old, it only seemed as if they wanted to make my life a living hell. Some advice that Scott gave to me that I now tell people today revolves around the controllable and uncontrollable aspects of our lives. Here is what you can control: yourself. So, when you have no impact or chance to change something, it is better to learn now to just deal with it, instead of clouding your head with the stress that comes from something you cannot control. For instance, regardless of how much I disagreed with the amount of freedom given to me as a sophomore in high school, instead of complaining and building up my frustration, I decided to go into my limitations with the best possible attitude. As this tactic was one of the hardest things to do, I was able to go throughout my day feeling way more satisfied because I had not wasted my energy on something that I knew wasn't going to change. Don't let yourself get caught up in the uncontrollable.

Since football leadership, I was constantly told about the power of culture and how it can impact the efficiency and surroundings you put yourself in. I never quite got to see what was talked about executed on our football team, and after that I dismissed the idea of how culture is so imperative to success. This ties in to the analogy that you cannot hang out at a barber shop and not get a haircut eventually, meaning that depending on who you surround yourself with, you will soon find yourself acting like them and living a similar lifestyle. Once I got the chance to work at Chateau with Scott, I finally got to see this importance of culture and how it can drive a company. The business knowledge that has been given to me through my time working at Chateau and Whitehead Associates has been an experience that I will take so much from. To be able to finally not only hear about culture but see what Scott had repetitively said to us being applied in his own workspace was an aha moment for me. The type of leadership it takes to successfully have people buy into the same vision and share a common goal is one of the most impressive attributes that Scott has shown me. When he lives his life this way, the people around him pick up on it and can treat others the way he does.

I hope that by surrounding myself with people who share faith-based morals and are here to serve other people, I can rest satisfied knowing I have served my purpose here in the time that I have.

—Jack

Open Up: Communicating with Your Kids

One of the best results of spending time with your kids is the chance to really talk with them. Communicating is a skill, and it's something we can all find ways to improve.

When kids get to be about eleven or twelve years old, they stop viewing you as a superhero and start seeing you as a real person. When you open up and have real conversations with them, they

As parents, we tend to spend a lot of time asking questions. "How was school?" "Do you have any homework?" "What did you eat for lunch?" But communicating is a two-way street. It's just as important to open up and share your day with your kids as it is for them to share stories about their day. Tell a funny story from lunch with your friends, talk to them about an interesting project you're doing at work, or discuss what's going on in current events.

get to know you even better. These conversations are a great way to pass on your own values to your kids and set a foundation for them as adults.

Spending Time as a Mentor

Quality time is just as important in the mentor/mentee relationship. As a mentor, you're not around all the time, so you want to make the time you have together impactful. Start off with an hour a week, maybe two. Find an activity that the child enjoys and do that together to begin opening up the lines of communication. Then it's a little easier to be a part of their life at other times too. It only takes a few seconds to send a text or reply to a post on social media. The timing is a little easier, because the child doesn't require all the time from a mentor that they would from a parent. They know you're outside of the family, but at the same time, they know you're there for them and you're a person they can turn to when they have a problem.

I was part of a Bible study Scott had organized with friends of mine from my school, and in addition, we had begun to meet more one-on-one with the upcoming trials of high school staring me in the face. I had many falls throughout high school where Scott was always there to pick me back up, and all the while he was building the confidence of one of the least confident kids you'll ever meet. My senior year started like most problems in high school with a girl. I had a long relationship that I admittedly ruined with a few large mistakes. This was a time when many people in my life turned their back on me and I was at a low in many aspects from confidence to happiness, but as I said earlier, Scott was always there with a hand outreached to pick me up and help me move on. This had a big impact on me considering that I had lied to him like I had to many others, and he had every reason to turn his back on me like many others did. This really taught me the Christian principle of forgiveness that is so commonly taught but so rarely practiced. Scott has taught me to appreciate myself as much as I self-loathed, and after seeing him two to three times a week pretty consistently for a year, slowly I have become more confident in myself and have slowly become less reliant on distractions to maintain my state of well-being.

So many mentors miss the mark, trying to over-advise young adults and impose their "wisdom," but something they could all learn from Scott is that sometimes we just need a friend, a good, consistent friend. In this stage of life, friends can be unreliable, and having an older friend who is always there to listen and help with a lot of patience can make life-changing differences in people's lives.

—*Ben*

I've never really expressed my feelings to someone, and I didn't think Scott would be the first person to open me up. The very first time we hung out alone I ended up breaking down and telling everything to this man I had only known for a few weeks. That's when the connection started. It hasn't even been a year since we've met, and my life has already been greatly impacted. Scott isn't just a "mentor." He's my friend and is someone I know I can always count on. I look forward to the remaining three years of high school with him and never plan on that friendship ending.

—*Rives*

Spending time with your kids and mentees pays dividends over time as you build a strong foundation of self-confidence and trust in them and create relationships that last through the teenage years and into adulthood. Over time, you'll realize you've become their friend and you've built a great relationship. This relationship, built on love and trust, will last a lifetime.

Conclusion

As I said earlier in this book, I hope that at the end of your parenting and mentoring journey, your young adult will be off on their own creating success and giving back to the community, and you will find that they have become one of your best friends. This is a direct result of all these lessons—time spent, faith-building, setting expectations. But at some point, the relationship shifts from one in which you support them to one in which they inspire you, motivate you, and begin to teach you new things. They'll remind you what you may have forgotten and help you find the excitement you might have lost. They will recreate that excitement in you.

It's pretty amazing how the circle of life is true: God puts you in a child's life, and God gives you the gift of being able to mentor, love, and grow that life into something that then benefits your life in a way you never expected. It's a natural evolution, and the friendships that develop (not only with your own kids, but with the kids you mentor) expand from discussions about parents, grades, and substances to conversations about real-life issues for adults, such as careers, marriages, kids, job changes, spiritual battles, and spiritual warfare. The conversations evolve in an incredible way from the mundane—when you have to continually use the power of guardrails to keep your child or a mentee in the center of the road—to relationships that are just fulfilling, which is a wonderful gift and reward from God. You won't even realize it's happening until one day you wake up and have an amazing conversation with your now adult and think, *Wow—it did happen.*

Doing right by children for the first fifteen to eighteen years and raising a contributing world citizen translates into a lifetime of joy and confidence beyond their childhood. They then build the next generation in a way that makes both you and God proud.

Now that my kids are older and long past being in my Sunday school classes, I still enjoy mentoring, because when it's your gift and passion, it transcends everything else. My plan is to continue not only mentoring but sharing what I know by speaking to groups of parents. Moms and dads are the most important people by a large multiple in kids' lives, so if you can say something to a parent that changes their parenting trajectory, then you've really made a difference in the life of a kid. I hope that my speaking, combined with the lessons I've shared in this book, can help foster the growth of generations.

And I have one more goal: I want to be one hundred years old and still be able to relate to teens, share advice, and help them with their issues. I'm still doing pretty well at this in my fifties, so I'm hopeful I can still do it in another few decades. Wish me luck!

For more information about Scott Whitehead, please visit *www.pillarsofsupportbook.com*

Lightning Source UK Ltd.
Milton Keynes UK
UKHW011419020323
417930UK00004B/269

9 781088 064351